Understanding the Prophetic

Biblical Insights Into The Prophetic Ministry

Archbishop Nicholas Duncan-Williams

Contents

Introduction

As you embark on a journey through the pages of this book, let me challenge any preconceived notions about the role of the prophet in our times.

Despite what many may believe, the office of the New Testament prophet is not a relic of the past but rather a vital force that continues to shape the Church. With its roots in the revelation and teachings of the Apostle Paul, prophecy remains a powerful gift of God for unlocking divine wisdom and guidance in a world that so desperately needs it.

God used prophets in Old Testament times to speak to Israel. How much more is He not using prophets for us in the New Covenant to impart divine wisdom and guidance? This very question has inspired me to pen these pages and shed light on the office and function of the Prophetic in these end times.

I've had the privilege to be used by God in the gift of prophecy over decades of ministry to world leaders and among the most impoverished. Allow me to share a few remarkable instances where the Holy Spirit spoke through me, delivering messages of significance to influential leaders.

During the term of General Abdulsalami Abubakar, I stood before Chief Olusegun Obasanjo and prophesied that he would ascend to the presidency of Nigeria. Against all odds and contrary to prevailing circumstances, Chief Obasanjo assumed Nigeria's highest office just six months later. The fulfillment of this prophecy was a testament to the faithfulness and sovereignty of God.

Not only did I have the honor of speaking prophetic words to Chief Obasanjo, but I was also commissioned by the Lord to deliver a message to him that he had one more term to serve as the president of Nigeria. Miraculously, he triumphed in the subsequent election, affirming the accuracy of the prophetic word spoken to him.

It is essential to clarify that throughout Chief Obasanjo's eight-year term and beyond, I sought no personal favor or advantage from him. My purpose was solely to serve as a vessel to deliver God's messages without compromising the integrity of the prophetic ministry.

In addition to Chief Obasanjo, I have been humbled to prophesy to President Felix Tshisekedi of the Democratic Republic of Congo and various other presidents, unveiling the outcomes of their presidential aspirations before they assumed office. These moments witness God's extraordinary ways of communicating His divine plans through His servants.

During a pivotal moment in Kenya's political landscape, William Ruto, with a passion to become the Head of State to help his people, approached me seeking divine guidance. God gave me a Word, assuring him that his time would come but first, he must serve under the leadership of Jomo Kenyatta.

William Ruto heeded this message and followed my counsel, and in due time, his patience and faithfulness were rewarded as he rose to take the mantle of power after Kenyatta.

I will never forget when a young Pastor approached me with a burning passion and enthusiasm, describing in vivid detail a dream where he saw himself distributing an abundance of shear butter to his congregants. Intrigued and eager to help him understand the spiritual significance of his vision, I delved into scripture and uncovered a powerful truth about butter in scriptures:

Just as I was in the days of my prime, when the friendly counsel of God was over my tent; When the Almighty was yet with me, when my children were around me; When my steps were bathed with cream, And the rock poured out rivers of oil for me. Job 29:4-6

I explained in detail the importance of allowing the Word of God to be the foundation of one's life and how obedience to His Word leads to abundance and prosperity. By a divine prophetic unction, I then instructed the young Pastor to share with his congregation the principles of faith, obedience, and prosperity as outlined in the Word of God.

The young Pastor followed my counsel and witnessed incredible results. The Word of God began to take root in the hearts of his flock, leading to an outpouring of abundance and blessings that surpassed their wildest dreams.

As I reflect on the relevance of the prophetic ministry in our present times, I am convinced that God has not ceased to call and anoint individuals to execute this vital ministry in the body of Christ. Despite the challenges and misconceptions surrounding the prophetic ministry, there are still many who are truly called to serve in this capacity.

However, I am not oblivious to the fact that there are also individuals who falsely claim to be prophets, causing confusion and discord in the body of Christ. Sadly, some have hijacked this sacred office for their own selfish gain, causing much harm and damage to those around them.

I have also observed that some true prophets operate as if we are still under the Old Testament dispensation. They seem unaware that God has instituted a new format for the prophetic ministry under the New Testament.

In writing this book, my primary focus is to equip and empower those who have been genuinely called into the office of the prophet.

My heart desires to help them effectively carry out their ministry and become a source of blessing to the body of Christ, and the nations of the world. With the proper guidance, the prophetic ministry can continue to be a powerful force in our 21st-century world.

Undoubtedly, we are living in the last days as the signs are unmistakable. However, while the world appears to be trapped in a cycle of repetitive history, the Church is called to a higher purpose.

We have two crucial responsibilities in these end times.

Firstly, we must actively reach out to the lost and bring them into the Kingdom of God. Millions of people live without Christ, and it is our duty to intervene and show them the way to salvation. Jesus said that the harvest is plentiful, but the laborers are few. We need more workers to gather those who will be saved when they call on the name of the Lord.

Secondly, we must encourage believers to grow spiritually and not remain stagnant in their faith. Many believers have accepted Christ but are not growing in Him as they should. After years of being born again, they still live their lives in a carnal way, ignoring the scriptures' exhortations. We must encourage them to live spiritually and fulfill the purpose for which God has called them.

The devil's plan is to deceive and lead astray those who have expressed faith in the Lord Jesus, as well as those who are not yet saved. He uses various tactics to achieve this goal, including creating false beliefs and doctrines, promoting false teachers and prophets, and fostering an environment of unbelief and skepticism.

In the Bible, the Apostle Peter and Apostle Paul both warned of the deception that would be prevalent in the last days. Therefore, as believers, we must be vigilant and discerning, test everything against the truth of God's Word, and remain steadfast in our faith.

Knowing this first: that scoffers will come in the last days, walking according to their own lusts, and saying, "Where is the promise of His coming? For since the fathers fell asleep, all things continue as they were from the beginning of creation." 2 Peter 3:3-4

Now the Spirit expressly says that in latter times some will depart from the faith, giving heed to deceiving spirits and doctrines of demons, ² speaking lies in hypocrisy, having their own conscience seared with a hot iron, ³ forbidding to marry, and commanding to abstain from foods which God created to be received with thanksgiving by those who believe and know the truth. 1 Timothy 4:1-3

Paul was serious when he warned us about the doctrines of devils. These wolves in sheep's clothing aren't just lurking outside the church doors. They're already inside, posing as believers and preying on the vulnerable.

These so-called ministers have knowledge of the Bible, but they lack true wisdom and revelation of the Word of God. They're all about hooking desperate and troubled people on their supposed solutions, but they're leading them down a dangerous path.

Now, I know some of these folks mean well. They're gifted and they have good hearts. But their understanding of the prophetic ministry is leading them astray from what God expects.

That's why I wrote this book, to teach a balance between the Old Testament Prophetic ministry and the New Testament Prophetic ministry. They may have a lot in common, but there are key differences that modern-day prophets need to understand. We can't just go back to the ways God dealt with the Children of Israel under the Old Covenant.

There's a verse hidden in Acts chapter 18 that gives me the spiritual courage to speak out as a spiritual father to people all over the world about the direction and operation of the prophetic.

Now a certain Jew named Apollos, born at Alexandria, an eloquent man and mighty in the Scriptures, came to Ephesus. This man had been instructed in the way of the Lord; and being fervent in spirit, he spoke and taught accurately the things of the Lord, though he knew only the baptism of John. So he began to speak boldly in the synagogue. When Aquila and Priscilla heard him, they took him aside and explained to him the way of God more accurately. Acts 18:24-26

Apollos was a learned man with a thorough knowledge of the Scriptures. He preached with great passion and taught about Jesus accurately. But he didn't know about the Baptism of the Holy Spirit for it says that he knew only the baptism of John.

Thankfully, the wise and experienced Aquila and Priscilla stepped in to help him out. As mature Christians and helpers in Christ, they weren't afraid to teach Apollos what he needed to know. And Apollos had the humility to listen and learn from them.

This is a valuable lesson for all believers, even today. It's important to accept guidance from those who are wiser and more experienced than us. And as for me, I hope to play a similar role as Priscilla and Aquila in offering instruction and guidance to my fellow believers.

My ultimate goal is to help you become as effective as God wants you to be. I don't want to see the ministry that God has given you discredited. It's so easy to get caught up in our own agendas and plans, but when we seek guidance and wisdom from those who have wisdom from years and decades of experience, we can be sure that we are on the right path.

So, let's walk together through this book and discover the truths and lessons it has to offer. I believe that as we journey together, we will grow in wisdom and understanding, and be better equipped to fulfill the calling that God has placed on our lives. Welcome aboard, my friends!

Chapter 1

What is a Prophet?

A prophet is one who sees the invisible, hears the inaudible, and speaks the unspoken. - John A. Widtsoe

Imagine walking through a crowded marketplace in ancient times, the smells of spices and fresh produce wafting through the air, the sound of vendors haggling with customers ringing in your ears.

As you make your way through the throngs of people, you notice a man standing on a soapbox, speaking with a voice that cuts through the noise of the market. He's not trying to sell anything, but rather, he's speaking of things to come. He's a prophet, one who has been given divine insight into the future by God.

Throughout history, prophets have emerged to deliver messages of warning, guidance, and hope to their fellow human beings. They have been revered and respected but also ridiculed and persecuted for the messages they bring. And yet, their words have stood the test of time, serving as a guide for generations to come.

But what exactly is a prophet? According to the Merriam-Webster dictionary, a prophet is *"one who utters divinely inspired revelations; one gifted with more than ordinary spiritual and moral insight; one who foretells future events; an effective or leading spokesman for a cause, doctrine, or group."*

In other words, a prophet is someone who has been granted a special insight into the workings of the world, a glimpse into the future, and a message to share with their fellow human beings. The source of their revelations is God.

The Different Hebrew Terms for Prophet

In the Hebrew language, several different words are used to describe a prophet. Each word carries its own nuanced meaning and understanding of what it means to be a prophet. Understanding these different terms can help us gain a deeper understanding of the role of a prophet in Hebrew society and their significance in the Bible.

Seer. The term "ro'eh," which means "seer," is used in the Old Testament to refer to a specific type of prophet. It is first used in 1 Samuel 9:9 to describe Samuel, a prophet in the early days of Israel. The term "ro'eh" comes from the Hebrew word "to see," and it is used to describe someone who can see things that others cannot.

The "seer" had a close relationship with God and understood His ways and plans. As a result, people would consult with the "seer" to ascertain God's will. However, as time went on, the term "ro'eh" was replaced by the term "nabi," which means "prophet" and comes from the Hebrew root "to call." The term "prophet" emphasizes the idea that the prophet is called by God to deliver His message to the people.

Hozeh. The Hebrew term "hozeh" is a synonym of "ro'eh," both of which mean "seer." However, "hozeh" comes from a rarer Hebrew term, which means "to see in a vision." It is mentioned in 2 Samuel 24:11 and Amos 7:12.

Nabi. The Hebrew term "nabi'" is the most commonly used term in the Old Testament to describe a prophet. Its exact etymology is uncertain, but it is believed to be a cognate of the Akkadian verb "nabu" meaning "to call" and Arabic "naba'a" meaning "to announce."

This term is used over 300 times and describes a person who speaks for God to His people. In essence, a prophet is called by YHWH to convey His messages to His people. This is well illustrated in the relationship between Moses, Aaron, and Pharaoh in Exodus 4:10-16 and 7:1, as well as in the prophetic calls of Amos, Jeremiah, and Ezekiel.

All three terms – seer, hozeh, and nabi - are used for the prophet's office in 1 Chr. 29:29; Samuel– *Ro'eh*; Nathan – *Nabi'*; and Gad– *Hozeh.*

'ish ha - 'elohim. In the Old Testament, the phrase 'ish ha-'elohim, which means "man of God," is used to refer to a speaker for God and is often used interchangeably with the term "prophet." This designation is given to individuals who have a special calling and relationship with God and are called upon to speak on His behalf.

The term "man of God" is used to describe a wide range of individuals, from Elijah and Elisha to unnamed prophets who appear briefly in the biblical narrative. It is a powerful and

3

evocative term, signifying a person whom God has set apart for a special purpose.

Based on these Hebrew words for a prophet, we can conclude that a prophet, as described in the Scriptures, is a person God chose to convey His message to the world. Essentially, a prophet serves as a messenger of God, and their words come directly from Him. This definition aligns with the words of the Apostle Peter.

And so we have the prophetic word confirmed, which you do well to heed as a light that shines in a dark place, until the day dawns and the morning star rises in your hearts; knowing this first, that no prophecy of Scripture is of any private interpretation, for prophecy never came by the will of man, but holy men of God spoke as they were moved by the Holy Spirit. 2 Peter 1:19-21

The New Testament Term for Prophet

The Greek term *prophetes* is the equivalent of the Old Testament *nabi* and is rendered in English as "prophet." The term's basic definition is "to speak forth" - a genuine prophet is someone who speaks on behalf of God.

In essence, the New Testament terms for prophets emphasize that they are individuals who are sent forth with a divine message and are empowered by the Holy Spirit to proclaim it with boldness and clarity.

A Summary of the Role of The Prophet

- Prophecy, in its classical form, is conveyed by a prophet or a seer who acts in the name of God.
- The prophet is a messenger who delivers a specific message from God to individuals, families, groups, communities, or nations.
- They usually serve as heralds, town criers, announcers, or interpreters, mediating between God and humanity.
- If a prophet attempts to evade their mission, like Jonah or Elijah, God gives them an opportunity to repent and return to the prophetic office.
- ·God reveals himself to prophets in dreams or visions, with Moses being the only Old Testament prophet to see God through a burning bush. As a result, Moses is considered the greatest prophet.

Then He said, "Hear now My words: If there is a prophet among you, I, the Lord, make Myself known to him in a vision; I speak to him in a dream. Not so with My servant Moses; He is faithful in all My house. I speak with him face to face, even plainly, and not in dark sayings; And he sees the form of the Lord. Deuteronomy 34:7-10

The Wise Grandfather

Although it's essential for any true student of the Bible to understand these various Biblical uses and definitions of the term prophet, we must not neglect the simplicity of the Word of God.

So we end this chapter with a story about a young boy curious about the role of a prophet in the Bible. He asked his Sunday school teacher, "What is a prophet, and why were they important in the Bible?"

The teacher responded with a lengthy and scholarly explanation. The boy listened attentively but struggled to understand the complexity of the answer.

Later that day, the boy visited his grandfather, a wise and respected man in the church. He posed the same question to his grandfather, who simply replied, "A prophet is like a mailman. They deliver a message from God to people."

The boy's eyes lit up with understanding, and he exclaimed, "Oh, I get it! Prophets are like God's messengers!" His grandfather smiled and nodded, pleased with the simplicity of his explanation.

From that day on, the boy had a newfound appreciation for the role of a prophet in the Bible. He understood that they were chosen by God to deliver important messages to people.

Chapter 2

Prophetic Ministry in the Old Testament

A prophet is someone who speaks the truth, no matter what the cost.

- Brennan Manning

The stories of the Old Testament are some of the most compelling and captivating narratives in human history. They are tales of heroism, tragedy, and divine intervention, chronicling the journey of the Hebrew people from their time in Egypt to their conquest of the Promised Land.

Their story is one of faith and struggle, triumphs and failures, and the enduring power of God's promises. And at the heart of it all are the people of Israel, the descendants of Abraham, who lived their lives under the watchful eye of Almighty God.

The journey of the Israelites began In Egypt, where they lived for 430 years, some of which were spent in slavery after a

Pharaoh withdrew the privileges they had enjoyed under Joseph. However, God promised to deliver them from bondage and did so through the leadership of Moses, performing miraculous interventions to ensure their safety.

After their deliverance, the people of Israel embarked on their journey through the wilderness as God's special people. However, the journey to the Promised Land was not without hardships and challenges. Fraught with danger and uncertainty, they encountered numerous enemies along the way.

Yet, time and time again, they emerged victorious, not through their own strength but through God's intervention. Every nation that dared to confront them in battle was defeated by the hand of the Lord in ways that defied human understanding.

After the death of Moses, God chose Joshua to lead the Israelites into the Promised Land, a daunting task that required not only military prowess but unwavering faith. Through Joshua's leadership and the Lord's miraculous interventions, the Israelites overcame seemingly insurmountable obstacles, including the crossing of the Jordan River and the conquest of Jericho.

Their triumphs were a testament to the power of faith and the unwavering love of God. And even in their darkest moments, as they faced defeat and despair, they knew they were not alone, for the Lord was with them every step of the way.

It is of the LORD'S mercies that we are not consumed, because his compassions fail not. They are new every morning: great is thy faithfulness. Lamentations 3:22-23

After Joshua's death, the Israelites entered a period of transition and uncertainty. They no longer had a single leader like Moses or Joshua to guide them, and the land of Canaan was filled with powerful enemies and potential threats.

In this time of need, God raised up a series of Judges to lead His people, men, and women whom He had chosen and anointed with His Spirit. These Judges were not traditional kings but rather individuals with courage, wisdom, and faith who could inspire and guide the Israelites in times of crisis.

Yet despite many remarkable achievements of the Judges, the period of the Judges was also marked by chaos, violence, and moral decay. It says in Judges 21:25, *"In those days there was no king in Israel; everyone did what was right in his own eyes."* The Israelites were plagued by internal strife and conflict, and they struggled to maintain their faith and obedience to God.

However, even amid this darkness, God remained faithful to His people. He continued to call and anoint Judges, such as Deborah and Barak, who were able to lead the Israelites to victory over their enemies.

And ultimately, the period of the Judges paved the way for establishing the monarchy. The people desired a king, and Samuel anointed Saul and later David as Israel's first and second kings, respectively.

What we learn from the ways of God under the old covenant is that God spoke to His people through chosen men and prophets of God. They were messengers of God that guided the Hebrew people on their journey in Egypt to their conquest of the Promised Land.

Their story is a tale of divine intervention, faith, and struggle. It's a testament to the enduring power of God's promises and the unbreakable spirit of His people.

The Prophet Samuel

When we talk about the prophet Samuel, we must begin with Hannah's story of faith, and sacrifice. She was a devout woman who longed for a child, but she could not conceive for many years.

Finally, in her desperation, she turned to the Lord and made a vow, promising to dedicate her child to Him if He would grant her the gift of motherhood.

God heard Hannah's prayers and blessed her with a son, whom she named Samuel. True to her word, Hannah gave Samuel back to God, bringing him to the temple to be raised by the priest Eli as a Nazarite.

Hannah's sacrifice was a profound demonstration of her faith and willingness to put God's will above her desires. She could have clung tightly to Samuel and kept him for herself, but instead, she recognized that he was a gift from God and entrusted him to His care.

Although Samuel was not raised by his parents, he grew up as a mighty prophet and leader known for his unwavering devotion to God. Hannah's faith and sacrifice were pivotal in shaping Samuel's character and preparing him for his important role in Israel's history.

It says in 1 Samuel 3:19-21:

And Samuel grew, and the Lord was with him and let none of his words fall to the ground. And all Israel from Dan to Beer-

sheba knew that Samuel had been established as a prophet of the Lord. Then the Lord appeared again in Shiloh. For the Lord revealed Himself to Samuel in Shiloh by the word of the Lord.

As Israel's history unfolded, its relationship with God faced many challenges and struggles. At one point, they began to turn away from the Lord and sought to emulate the nations around them by demanding a king to rule over them.

This was a significant departure from God's original plan for Israel to be a nation led by judges called and appointed by God. Nevertheless, God saw fit to grant the people's request, and He chose the prophet Samuel to anoint the first king of Israel.

The man chosen was Saul, who initially showed great promise as a leader but ultimately proved unfaithful to God. After Saul's reign ended, Samuel anointed a new king, a young shepherd boy named David.

David's reign would be one of the most significant in Israel's history. He was a man after God's own heart, and under his leadership, Israel experienced a period of great prosperity and spiritual renewal.

Despite David's many flaws and failings, he remained steadfast in his devotion to God, and his legacy would be felt for generations to come. He was the forefather of Jesus Christ, who would be known as the King of Kings and Lord of Lords.

Two Groups of Prophets

The distinction between the two groups of prophets in the Bible reveals an interesting aspect of the prophetic tradition.

The prophets of Acts, including Samuel, Nathan, Elijah, and Elisha, were recognized for their deeds rather than words. Their stories were recorded in the history books of the Bible, portraying their actions and the miracles they performed in the name of God.

The classical prophets, also known as the writing prophets or the book prophets, were known for their powerful words and profound insights into God's plan for humanity. These prophets, including Isaiah, Jeremiah, and Ezekiel, are considered to have played a crucial role in shaping the beliefs of the Jewish people. Their prophecies were recorded in books that bear their names and are regarded as some of the most significant works in the Hebrew Scriptures.

The classical prophets lived during a period of great upheaval in the history of the Jewish people between the 8th and 5th centuries B.C., known as the Return-to-Zion era. They were called upon to warn the people of impending disaster and to offer hope and comfort in the face of adversity. Their messages were often difficult to hear, as they spoke of God's judgment and the need for repentance. But they also spoke of a future restoration and a renewed covenant with God, offering a vision of hope for the future.

Together, these two groups of prophets represent a rich tradition of prophecy in the Bible, revealing the diverse ways in which God speaks to humanity and guides us on our spiritual journey.

Major and Minor Prophets

In addition to being categorized as "prophets of acts" and "classical prophets," the prophets of the Hebrew Scriptures were also divided into two groups based on the length and scope of their prophetic books: major prophets and minor prophets.

The major prophets, including Isaiah, Jeremiah, Lamentations, Ezekiel, and Daniel, are referred to as such because their prophetic books are longer and more comprehensive in their coverage of God's message.

Jeremiah's book is considered the longest in the Hebrew Scriptures, containing 52 chapters that cover a range of topics, including the judgment of Judah and the surrounding nations, the fall of Jerusalem, and the hope for future restoration.

On the other hand, the minor prophets are so-called not because their messages are any less important but because their books are shorter and more specific in scope. The twelve minor prophets, including Hosea, Joel, Amos, Obadiah, Jonah, Micah, Nahum, Habakkuk, Zephaniah, Haggai, Zechariah, and Malachi, each focus on a particular message from God, such as judgment, repentance, or restoration.

Despite their differences in length and scope, the messages of the prophets, whether major or minor, all point to the same overarching themes of God's sovereignty, righteousness, and love for His people. Their prophecies serve as a reminder of God's faithfulness throughout history and a call to trust and obey Him in every circumstance.

Titles of Old Testament Prophets

The prophets that God chose to speak His words to the people of Israel were known by various titles, each reflecting a different aspect of their role and mission.

The Man of God– As we see in 1 Samuel 9:6; 1 Kings 12:22, the title "The Man of God" was not just a mere label or a name given to the prophets of the Old Testament, but it represented a way of life. These prophets were not just messengers who delivered God's messages to His people, but they lived and breathed the ways of God. They were the ones who modeled the behavior and character that God expected from His people.

The Seers– This title bestowed upon the prophets is a testament to their extraordinary gift of foresight and insight, given to them directly from the Lord. These individuals had the unique ability to see beyond the present and into the future, providing invaluable guidance and direction to the people of their time. Through visions and divine revelations, they could discern God's will and communicate it to the people. We read about seers in 1 Samuel 9:9; 2 Chronicles 33:18; 35:15; 2 Samuel 24:11; Amos 7:12; Isaiah 29:10.

The Interpreters– As we read in Isaiah 43:27, prophets were also called Interpreters or teachers. The prophets were the interpreters of the Law of the Lord. They interpreted the nation's history in the light of the Word of God.

The Messengers of the Lord– In Isaiah 37: 9 and Malachi 3:1, we see the title *Messenger of the Lord* used in reference to the office of the prophet. The prophets were not just ordinary messengers; they were divine emissaries specially chosen by God to convey His messages to the people.

The Servants– The prophets were called the Servants of Jehovah in Haggai 2:23. They were His slaves - love slaves - to the will and service of God.

The Prophets–Hosea 12:10. The most widely recognized title given to these chosen individuals is that of a prophet. As public expounders and preachers of the Word of the Lord, they spoke under the guidance and inspiration of the Spirit. As 2 Peter 1:21 states, *"Holy men of God spoke as they were moved of the Holy Spirit."* Their prophecies were conveyed through preaching and prediction, representing God's Word to Israel. Upholding the righteousness of the Law, the holiness and mercy of God, and Divine sovereignty over the nations, they also admonished people for their sinful ways.

These prophets were empowered by God's Spirit and led by Him in their divine mission to deliver God's message to people who had little regard for Him. This truth is evidenced in multiple Bible passages, such as those in the books of Numbers and Ezekiel.

So the Lord *said to Moses: "Gather to Me seventy men of the elders of Israel, whom you know to be the elders of the people and officers over them; bring them to the tabernacle of meeting, that they may stand there with you. Then I will come down and talk with you there. I will take of the Spirit that is upon you and will put the same upon them; and they shall bear the burden of the people with you, that you may not bear it yourself alone.* Numbers 11:16-17

So the Spirit lifted me up and took me away, and I went in bitterness, in the heat of my spirit; but the hand of the Lord was strong upon me. Ezekiel 3:14

The Work of the Old Testament Prophets

Before the establishment of the monarchy and Israel's entry into the Promised Land, there were already prophets. However, the office of the prophet became more prominent during and after the divided kingdom period, when the tribes of Israel were split into the northern kingdom of Israel and the southern kingdom of Judah.

During these few centuries, from around 800 B.C. to 450 B.C., all of the "writing prophets" - such as Isaiah, Jeremiah, Hosea, and others - lived and delivered their messages.

One of the prophets' primary themes was the consequences of obedience or disobedience to God's laws. The prophets warned that disobedience would bring severe consequences, while obedience would result in blessings.

Unfortunately, Israel, the nation God chose to be an example of the way of life, turned away from Him and worshipped pagan gods.

The prophets' message centered around the cyclical behavior of Israel: rebellion against God, punishment from God (including captivity), and restoration to God, ultimately bringing them back to their land.

As the mouthpieces of God, the prophets had the primary duty of delivering His message to His people in the historical context of what was happening among them.

Forth-telling and Foretelling

Two of the main functions of prophecy in the Old Testament were *forth-telling* and *foretelling*.

Forthtelling is the act of receiving insight into the will of God, and it is exhortative, challenging individuals to obey God's commands. This form of prophecy is closely related to preaching, as the prophet speaks on behalf of God to communicate His intentions for the present.

The prophet may frequently draw on the past to address current situations. This function of forth-telling includes exhortation, reproof, warning, edification, and assurance.

Foretelling involved foresight into the plan of God; it was predictive, either encouraging the righteous with God's promises or warning of impending judgment. In proclaiming God's message, the prophet sometimes revealed what pertained to the future.

Foretelling was mainly about the future of God's people, such as the prophecies of the destruction of Israel (Amos 8) and Judah (Jeremiah 22) due to their sins. Many prophetic books also contain oracles against surrounding nations, proclaiming judgment on Assyria, Babylon, Edom, Aram, Egypt, and other lands (Ezekiel 25-32, Jeremiah 46-52, Isaiah 13-23).

Contrary to popular opinion, foretelling was only a small part of the prophets' message. The prophets did more forth-telling. As God's chosen spokesmen, the prophets proclaimed God's message in oral, visual, or written form to the people. For this reason, a common expression used by the prophets was "Thus says the Lord."

Other Roles of Prophets

Prophets were God's Spokesmen. Their message can be seen in a three-fold function they had among the people of God in the Old Testament: as Preachers, Predictors, or Watchmen.

Prophets as Preachers. As preachers, they expounded and interpreted the Mosaic law to the nation. Their duty was to admonish, reprove, denounce sin, threaten with the terrors of judgment, call to repentance, and bring consolation and pardon. Rebuking sin and calling for repentance consumed far more of the prophets' time than any other feature of their work. The rebuke was driven home with predictions about the punishment God intended to send on those failing to heed the prophet's warning. An example is the case of Nineveh (cf. Jonah 3:4).

Prophets as Predictors. As Predictors, they announced the coming judgment, deliverance, and events relating to the Messiah and His kingdom. Predicting the future was never intended merely to satisfy man's curiosity but to demonstrate that God knows and controls the future and to give purposeful revelation.

A prediction given by a true prophet would be visibly fulfilled. The failure of the prediction to be fulfilled would indicate that the prophet had not spoken the word of Yahweh. In 1 Samuel 3:19, it is said of Samuel that the Lord was with him and let none of his prophetic words fail (lit., "fall to the ground").

Prophets as Watchmen: As watchmen, prophets watched over the people of Israel (Ezek. 3:17). Ezekiel stood as

18

a watchman on the walls of Zion, ready to sound a warning against religious apostasy.

He warned the people against political and military alliances with foreign powers, the temptation to become involved in idolatry and Canaanite cultic worship, and the danger of placing excessive confidence in religious formalism and sacrificial ritual.

Although prophets functioned in various ways to communicate God's message, they played a crucial role in Israel's religious system. Prophets in Israel served as royal diplomats or prosecuting attorneys, accusing the nation of breaking the Mosaic covenant.

Some directed their message to the southern kingdom, and others to the northern kingdom. Most ministered before the Babylonian Exile, but a few (Haggai, Zechariah, and Malachi) ministered after.

God's Message Through His Prophets

Elisha: Elisha kept King Jehoram informed of the movements of the army of the Arameans (Syrians). Elisha's information saved the Israelite army from ambush and destruction several times, and Aramean King Ben Hadad suspected treachery.

When he was informed that Elisha the Prophet was the source of Jehoram's information, Ben Hadad sent an army to capture him. God blinded this army and gave them into the hand of Elisha (2 Kings 6:8-23).

Isaiah: The primary message of the book of Isaiah to the world is that there is indeed a Savior, the Messiah, who has humbly, painfully, and gloriously won salvation for sinners and for all who would trust in him (Isa. 4:2; 7:14; 9:6–7; 11:1–5; 42:1–4; 52:13–53:12; 61:1–3). Death is swallowed up, and our reproach is removed (25:8).

Isaiah, being sensitive to the decay in his society, also foresaw its inevitable collapse. However, he also knew and presented an alternative to tragedy: the survival of his people depended on their renewed acceptance of ancient moral demands.

By returning to God, they could be saved from destruction. As he spoke on behalf of God, Isaiah aimed to redirect his people towards conduct that was acceptable to the God they had alienated and save them from impending disaster.

Isaiah warned and pleaded with the people to change their ways. He became despondent only because his efforts did not yield any results. The people appeared determined to self-destruct, and he witnessed their sickening destiny unfolding before him.

Nevertheless, Isaiah assured Hezekiah that God would rescue Judah from the Assyrians led by Sennacherib, who had laid siege to Jerusalem (2 Kings 19:20-34).

Jeremiah: Jeremiah lived and prophesied during the sixth century B.C., leading up to and following the exile of Judah to Babylon. Through his prophecy, Jeremiah revealed the rebellious hearts of God's people that ultimately led to their exile. This was a devastating event, as God's covenant promises to Abraham included the promise of the land of Canaan.

Despite the apparent unraveling of these promises, God's strong statements of judgment throughout the Book of Jeremiah were surpassed by his pledge of mercy. He was determined not to abandon his people, no matter how sinful they became. Jeremiah encouraged the Israelites to pursue sincerity instead of superficiality and tried to prevent Judah's decline in morality, which led to its downfall.

The radical problem of sin required a radical solution, which was nothing less than the Lord himself writing his law on the very hearts of his people. This is explained in Jeremiah 31:33-34 and compared to 2 Corinthians 3:6. At the climax of Jeremiah's ministry, God's determination to restore his people to himself was reassured in Jeremiah 30-33. Additionally, Jeremiah warned Judah in Chapter 37 not to trust in Pharaoh and in Chapter 42, after the destruction of Jerusalem, not to flee to Egypt to escape the Babylonians.

Ezekiel: Ezekiel expanded on the message of God's love and grace, fully explaining it in chapter 36 of his prophecy. This chapter contains all the promises of the gospel, including a promise of cleansing from sin through sprinkling clean water upon his people, as stated in verse 25: *"Then I will sprinkle clean water on you, and you shall be clean; I will cleanse you from all your filthiness and from all your idols."*

Ezekiel prophesied that the exiles from both Judah and Israel would return to Palestine, leaving none in the Diaspora. In the new age to come, a new covenant would be made with the restored house of Israel, and God would give them a new spirit and a new heart.

As we see in the following scripture, Ezekiel was told to go to his people, the House of Israel, who were in captivity:

Moreover he said unto me, Son of man, eat that thou findest; eat this roll, and go speak unto the house of Israel." and *"And he said unto me, Son of man, go, get thee unto the house of Israel, and speak with my words unto them,"* and *" And go, get thee to them of the captivity, unto the children of thy people, and speak unto them, and tell them.* (Ezekiel 3:1, 4, 11).

In fact, God plainly stated that He would require Ezekiel's blood if he didn't go and deliver the warning.

Son of man, I have made thee a watchman unto the house of Israel: therefore, hear the word at my mouth, and give them warning from me.

When I say unto the wicked, Thou shalt surely die; and thou givest him not warning, nor speakest to warn the wicked from his wicked way, to save his life; the same wicked man shall die in his iniquity; but his blood will I require at thine hand.

Yet if thou warn the wicked, and he turn not from his wickedness, nor from his wicked way, he shall die in his iniquity; but thou hast delivered thy soul.

Again, when a righteous man doth turn from his righteousness, and commit iniquity, and I lay a stumbling block before him, he shall die: because thou hast not given him warning, he shall die in his sin, and his righteousness which he hath done shall not be remembered; but his blood will I require at thine hand.

Nevertheless if thou warn the righteous man, that the righteous sin not, and he doth not sin, he shall surely live, because he is warned; also thou hast delivered thy soul. (Ezekiel 3:17-21).

It's important to remember what happened to Jonah when he tried to escape what God had told him to do. Similarly, God warned Ezekiel that he would be held responsible if he didn't go and give the warning. In fact, Ezekiel was told that he would be struck dumb except when God opened his mouth in prophetic utterances.

> *And I will make thy tongue cleave to the roof of thy mouth, that thou shalt be dumb, and shalt not be to them a reprover: for they are a rebellious house. But when I speak with thee, I will open thy mouth, and thou shalt say unto them, Thus saith the Lord GOD;* (Ezekiel 3:26-27).

In Ezekiel 36:24-27, God reaches out to His people as a nation and as individuals, laying bare their sins.

> *For I will take you from among the nations, gather you out of all countries, and bring you into your own land. Then I will sprinkle clean water on you, and you shall be clean; I will cleanse you from all your filthiness and from all your idols. I will give you a new heart and put a new spirit within you; I will take the heart of stone out of your flesh and give you a heart of flesh. I will put My Spirit within you and cause you to walk in My statutes, and you will keep My judgments and do them.*

Ezekiel 37 contains a message of restoration for a nation that had collapsed and lost the life of God. Ezekiel's prophetic ministry was to bring life back into a lifeless nation by proclaiming God's message. Ezekiel's vision of the dry bones represents the resurrection from the dead to life, and his message carried the hope of God bringing Israel back to Himself.

Lessons Learned

The prophets arose in Israel during times when Kings were leading the people astray, often by worshipping idols. About 65% of the prophets' utterances were forth-telling, speaking to the people of Israel about their lives in relation to God's covenant rather than making predictions about personal lives.

The prophet's messages to Israel followed a similar format: 1) you have sinned, 2) you must repent, 3) you will be judged if you do not repent, and 4) you will be restored after repentance.

Each prophet's message from God was unique and tailored to their specific context. For example, Daniel predicted the rise and fall of several ancient empires, Isaiah predicted Jesus' birth to a virgin (Isaiah 7:14,), and Amos claimed, *"This is what the Lord said"* (Amos 1:3,). The prophets not only revealed God's message but also made known His holiness, disdain for idolatry, and desire for Israel to repent.

These anointed vessels were often met with ridicule, mockery, and mistreatment, but they continued with their purpose, sharing the truth with God's people until Jesus came centuries later.

The Bible confirms that death was punishment for speaking falsely in God's name. Of all Old Testament prophecies, scholars estimate that less than 5% are about the New Covenant, less than 2% are directly about the Messiah, and less than 1% are about events that are still in the future for Christians today.

Therefore, Christians should be cautious when applying an Old Testament prophecy to themselves, as it is easy to misapply them.

Yet, the prophecies we should pay special attention to are the prophecies that point to the coming of a Messiah. The term "Messiah" is a Hebrew word that means "anointed one."

In the Old Testament, it refers to a special person who would be chosen by God to lead his people and deliver them from their enemies. Many of the Old Testament prophets spoke of this coming Messiah and described his attributes and the nature of his mission.

One of the most famous prophecies about the Messiah is found in Isaiah 53. This chapter describes the suffering and death of a servant of God who would be "pierced for our transgressions" and "crushed for our iniquities." The prophet also notes that this servant would bear the sins of many and make intercession for them before God.

Other prophets, such as Micah, spoke of the Messiah's birthplace, saying that he would be born in Bethlehem. Zechariah prophesied that the Messiah would enter Jerusalem riding on a donkey and that he would be betrayed for thirty pieces of silver.

All of these prophecies were fulfilled in the person of Jesus Christ. He was born in Bethlehem, rode into Jerusalem on a donkey, and was betrayed by one of his disciples for thirty pieces of silver. He also suffered and died on the cross, bearing the sins of all humanity and making intercession for us before God.

Thus, Christ is the culmination of the Old Testament. He is the fulfillment of all the prophecies and promises made by God through the prophets.

Chapter 3

Unique Experiences of Old Testament Prophets

The prophets of the Old Testament were men of fire and zeal, who were unafraid to speak out against injustice and corruption, and to call the people of God back to righteousness and faithfulness. - Billy Graham

As we dive deeper into the subject of prophetic ministry, it's important to distinguish between the practices of Old Testament prophets and Modern-day prophets. We need to understand this difference, so we don't simply mimic the methods used by the prophets of the Old Testament.

So, in this chapter, we explore the unique aspect of the lives of Old Testament prophets that isn't found in the New Testament. Though these practices were commonplace in the days of the Old Testament, there is no record of God commanding or expecting His prophets in the New Testament to engage in them.

By understanding these differences between Old Testament and modern-day prophetic practices, we can more fully embrace the unique calling God has placed on our lives.

The Prophet Elijah

The Old Testament is full of fascinating stories of prophets and their unique appearances and commands from God. One such example is Elijah.

> *And when the messengers returned to him, he said to them, "Why have you come back?" So they said to him, "A man came up to meet us, and said to us, 'Go, return to the king who sent you, and say to him, "Thus says the Lord: 'Is it because there is no God in Israel that you are sending to inquire of Baal-Zebub, the god of Ekron? Therefore you shall not come down from the bed to which you have gone up, but you shall surely die.'"'" Then he said to them, "What kind of man was it who came up to meet you and told you these words?" So they answered him, a hairy man wearing a leather belt around his waist." And he said, "It is Elijah the Tishbite." (2 Kings 1:5-8).*

Elijah wore a garment of hair and had a leather belt around his waist. In this Scripture, we read about messengers who encountered Elijah and reported back to their king, describing him as "a hairy man wearing a leather belt around his waist."

Although wearing a leather belt is unique to Elijah and should not be practiced today by legitimate prophets, Elijah's garment made of hair and his leather belt are significant in their symbolism. The hair garment, likely made of animal hair or coarse wool, was a sign of Elijah's humility and willingness to live a simple life.

The leather belt around his waist also symbolized Elijah's strength and his readiness to do battle. In ancient times, a leather belt was an essential part of a warrior's equipment, and it was worn to keep the sword and other weapons close at hand. By wearing a leather belt, Elijah was demonstrating his readiness to fight for God and his people.

Elijah ate from a bird. During the time of Elijah, Israel was facing a severe drought as a result of their disobedience to God's commands. In response to their disobedience, God sent Elijah to prophesy against the nation and to declare that there would be no rain until God gave the command.

As the drought progressed, God provided for Elijah's needs in an extraordinary way. He commanded the ravens to bring Elijah food each day, which sustained him during his time in the cave. This provision was significant because ravens were considered unclean birds and were not known for providing food to humans. Nevertheless, God used them to provide for Elijah's needs.

The fact that God used ravens to provide for Elijah is also symbolic of God's ability to work through unconventional means to provide for his people. Just as he used an unlikely source to provide for Elijah, he can also use unexpected sources to provide for us.

However, the story of Elijah eating from a bird is unique in the Old Testament and should not be mimicked by prophets today. It was a special provision made by God for Elijah during a time of great need, and it was not meant to be a regular practice.

The Prophet Elisha

And Elisha saw it, and he cried out, "My father, my father, the chariot of Israel and its horsemen!" So he saw him no more. And he took hold of his own clothes and tore them into two pieces. He also took up the mantle of Elijah that had fallen from him, and went back and stood by the bank of the Jordan. Then he took the mantle of Elijah that had fallen from him, and struck the water, and said, "Where is the Lord God of Elijah?" And when he also had struck the water, it was divided this way and that; and Elisha crossed over. 2 Kings 2:12–14.

Elisha wore Elijah's Mantle. The story of Elisha taking up Elijah's mantle is a significant event in the Old Testament that symbolizes the transfer of the prophetic office from Elijah to Elisha. In this story, Elijah is taken into heaven in a whirlwind, leaving behind his mantle, which Elisha picks up and uses to perform a miracle.

Elisha's taking up Elijah's mantle symbolizes his acceptance of the prophetic office and the spiritual inheritance that Elijah has passed on to him. By taking up the mantle, Elisha becomes Elijah's spiritual heir and continues the work of prophesying and declaring God's message to the people.

The mantle itself also holds symbolic significance in this story. In the Old Testament, the mantle was a cloak or robe worn by prophets and other important religious figures. It was seen as a symbol of their authority and anointing by God. By taking up Elijah's mantle, Elisha is continuing Elijah's work and stepping into his authority and anointing.

Furthermore, the miracle that Elisha performs with the mantle, parting the waters of the Jordan River, shows that he has inherited the same power and authority as Elijah. This miracle serves as a sign that God has chosen Elisha to continue the prophetic work that Elijah began.

It is important to note that using Elijah's mantle to transfer the prophetic office from Elijah to Elisha is a symbolic act, not a prescription for how we should transfer spiritual authority today. While the mantle held great significance in the Old Testament, it is not necessary or even appropriate to use it as a physical symbol of the transfer of authority today.

Instead, we can look to the spiritual principles behind this story, such as the importance of passing on spiritual inheritance and the authority that comes with it and apply those principles in appropriate ways in our own lives and ministries.

Ultimately, the transfer of spiritual authority is a matter of God's calling and empowerment, rather than any physical object or ritual.

Elisha made an ax head float. The story of Elisha making an ax head float in 2 Kings 6:1-7 is a remarkable example of God's concern for even the smallest things in our lives. In ancient times, an ax head was a valuable and essential tool, especially for those who worked with wood.

So, when one of the sons of the prophets accidentally dropped the borrowed ax head into the river while working on a new settlement, it was a disaster. Losing such a valuable tool would have been a massive setback for the group.

But Elisha, being a man of God, knew that the situation could be turned around. He asked the man where the ax head had fallen, and when he pointed it out, Elisha cut a stick and threw it into the water. To everyone's amazement, the ax head floated to the surface, allowing the man to retrieve it.

This miracle not only solved a practical problem for the sons of the prophets, but it also communicated a powerful message about God's character. It showed that God cares about the small worries of our lives and is willing to intervene on our behalf, even in seemingly insignificant matters like a lost ax head.

It also demonstrated Elisha's power and authority as a prophet of God and strengthened the faith of those who witnessed the miracle.

In our own lives, we can take comfort in the fact that God cares about even the smallest details of our lives. We can trust that He is always watching over us and working on our behalf, even in impossible or hopeless situations.

The story of Elisha and the ax head reminds us that God is a God of miracles and that nothing is too small or insignificant for Him to handle.

The Prophet Ezekiel

And you, son of man, take a sharp sword, take it as a barber's razor, and pass it over your head and your beard; then take scales to weigh and divide the hair.

You shall burn with fire one-third in the midst of the city, when the days of the siege are finished; then you shall take one-third and strike around it with the sword, and one-third you shall scatter in the wind: I will draw out a sword after them.

You shall also take a small number of them and bind them in the edge of your garment. Then take some of them again and throw them into the midst of the fire, and burn them in the fire. From there a fire will go out into all the house of Israel. Ezekiel 5:1-4

God told Ezekiel to shave his head and beard. In Ezekiel 5:1-4, God instructed the prophet Ezekiel to take a sharp sword, shave his head and beard, and divide his hair into thirds. While this may seem like an odd request, it had a deeper meaning.

The hair of Ezekiel was divided into thirds, with each third representing a different punishment that God would bring upon the people.

One-third of the hair was to be burned, symbolizing the destruction that would come upon the people when the Babylonians besieged the city.

Another third was to be struck with the sword, representing the violence that would take place within the city as people turned against each other in desperation. Finally, the remaining third was to be scattered to the wind, symbolizing the scattering of the people throughout the nations.

Through this unusual command, God communicated the severity of the punishment that the people of Jerusalem would face due to their disobedience and rebellion against Him. It was a vivid and dramatic way to convey a message that the people needed to take seriously.

The shaving of Ezekiel's head and beard also served as a powerful visual aid to get people's attention. It was a symbol of the seriousness of the situation and a warning of what was to come if they did not repent and turn back to God. This event demonstrated that God is not bound by human traditions or expectations and that He could use unconventional methods to convey His message.

Ultimately, the story of Ezekiel's shaved head serves as a reminder that God will go to great lengths to get our attention and call us back to Himself.

Ezekiel lay on his side for weeks at a time.

You also, son of man, take a clay tablet and lay it before you, and portray on it a city, Jerusalem. Lay siege against it, build a siege wall against it, and heap up a mound against it; set camps against it also, and place battering rams against it all around.

Moreover take for yourself an iron plate, and set it as an iron wall between you and the city. Set your face against it, and it shall be besieged, and you shall lay siege against it.

This will be a sign to the house of Israel. Lie also on your left side, and lay the iniquity of the house of Israel upon it. According to the number of the days that you lie on it, you shall bear their iniquity.

For I have laid on you the years of their iniquity, according to the number of the days, three hundred and ninety days; so you shall bear the iniquity of the house of Israel.

And when you have completed them, lie again on your right side; then you shall bear the iniquity of the house of Judah forty days. I have laid on you a day for each year. Ezekiel 4:1-6

Although Ezekiel's act of lying on his side for weeks may seem like a strange request from God, it carried a powerful message for the people of Israel. The prophet was instructed to lie on his left side for 390 days, bearing the iniquity of Israel, and then on his right side for 40 days, bearing the iniquity of Judah.

This was not merely a physical endurance test for Ezekiel, but a prophetic sign of the consequences of Israel's disobedience to God. The act of lying on his side symbolized the siege that was coming upon Jerusalem and the weight of the people's sin that would lead to their destruction.

Ezekiel's unusual act served as a vivid and unforgettable reminder to the people that their sin had serious consequences, and that God was not to be mocked. It was a call to repentance and a warning of the impending judgment if they did not turn from their wicked ways. In this way, Ezekiel's strange and extreme act served as a powerful testimony to God's holiness and justice.

Jeremiah was told he could not marry

The word of the Lord also came to me, saying, "You shall not take a wife, nor shall you have sons or daughters in this place." For thus says the Lord concerning the sons and daughters who are born in this place, and concerning their mothers who bore them and their fathers who begot them in this land:

"They shall die gruesome deaths; they shall not be lamented nor shall they be buried, but they shall be like refuse on the face of the earth. They shall be consumed by the sword and by famine, and their corpses shall be meat for the birds of heaven and for the beasts of the earth." Jeremiah 16:2-4

In Jeremiah 16:2-4, we see a unique commandment given to the prophet Jeremiah - he was told not to marry or have children. This may seem strange to us, but it was a symbolic act meant to show the people of Israel that God's judgment was coming upon them.

The death and destruction that would come upon the people would be so great that it would not be appropriate to bring children into the world to experience it.

This commandment was unique to Jeremiah and was not meant to be taken as a universal principle for all people. Instead, it was a specific message for a particular time and place. However, the story's symbolism can still be relevant to us today.

We can learn from Jeremiah's obedience to God's unique commands and recognize that sometimes God calls us to do things that may seem unusual or challenging. And we can trust that God has a purpose for everything He asks us to do, even if we may not fully understand it at the time.

The Prophet Hosea was told to marry a prostitute

When the Lord began to speak by Hosea, the Lord said to Hosea:
"Go, take yourself a wife of harlotry, and children of harlotry,
For the land has committed great harlotry

By departing from the Lord." So he went and took Gomer
the daughter of Diblaim, and she conceived and bore him a son.
Hosea 1:2-3

The story of Hosea being commanded to marry a prostitute may seem surprising, but it symbolizes God's relationship with Israel. Hosea's wife, Gomer represents Israel, who was unfaithful to God and had turned to other gods.

By marrying Gomer, Hosea showed his unwavering love and commitment to her, just as God continued to love and remain committed to Israel even in their disobedience.

The names of Hosea's children also carried an important message. Jezreel represented the judgment that was to come upon the house of Israel due to their disobedience. Lo-Ruhamah, meaning "not loved," represented the moment when God would temporarily remove His mercy from Israel. And Lo-Ammi, meaning "not my people," symbolized the moment when God would temporarily disown Israel.

The story of Hosea's marriage reminds us that God's love and commitment to His people are unwavering, even when they turn away from Him. However, it is essential to note that this was a unique situation and should not be taken as a model for marriage today.

Prophet Isaiah prophesied naked and barefoot

In the year that Tartan came to Ashdod, when Sargon the king of Assyria sent him, and he fought against Ashdod and took it, at the same time the Lord spoke by Isaiah the son of Amoz, saying, "Go, and remove the sackcloth from your body, and take your sandals off your feet."

And he did so, walking naked and barefoot. Then the Lord said, "Just as My servant Isaiah has walked naked and barefoot three years for a sign and a wonder against Egypt and Ethiopia, so shall the king of Assyria lead away the Egyptians as prisoners and the Ethiopians as captives, young and old, naked and barefoot, with their buttocks uncovered, to the shame of Egypt. Isaiah 20:1-4

Isaiah's unusual behavior of walking naked and barefoot for three years may seem inappropriate. Still, it was a symbolic act that God instructed him to perform as a sign and wonder against Egypt and Ethiopia.

This unique situation should not be taken as an example to follow. In ancient times, prophets were sometimes called to engage in symbolic acts to communicate God's message in a powerful way.

The prophecy was that just as Isaiah walked naked and barefoot, the people of Egypt and Ethiopia would be led away as prisoners, stripped of their dignity, and brought to shame.

This story reminds us that God's ways are not always easy to understand, but his messages are always powerful and meaningful, even when they are communicated through unconventional means.

Jeremiah Smashed Pots

This is what the Lord says: "Go and buy a clay jar from a potter. Take along some of the elders of the people and of the priests and go out to the Valley of Ben Hinnom, near the entrance of the Potsherd Gate. There proclaim the words I tell you, and say, 'Hear the word of the Lord, you kings of Judah and people of Jerusalem.

This is what the Lord Almighty, the God of Israel, says: Listen! I am going to bring a disaster on this place that will make the ears of everyone who hears of it tingle.

For they have forsaken me and made this a place of foreign gods; they have burned incense in it to gods that neither they nor their ancestors nor the kings of Judah ever knew, and they have filled this place with the blood of the innocent.

They have built the high places of Baal to burn their children in the fire as offerings to Baal—something I did not command or mention, nor did it enter my mind.

So beware, the days are coming, declares the Lord, when people will no longer call this place Topheth or the Valley of Ben Hinnom, but the Valley of Slaughter. Jeremiah 19:1-6

In Jeremiah 19:1-6, God commands Jeremiah to buy a clay jar from a potter and take it, along with some elders and priests, to the Valley of Ben Hinnom. There, he is to proclaim God's message to the people of Judah and Jerusalem, warning them of the disaster about to come upon them because of their idolatry and the shedding of innocent blood.

The people of Judah had turned away from God and started worshiping foreign gods, burning incense to gods they and their ancestors had never known. They had even gone so far as to sacrifice their own children to the false god Baal, something that God had never commanded or even imagined.

The Valley of Ben Hinnom had become a place of great wickedness and evil, and God would bring judgment upon the people for their sins. He warns them that the days are coming when the valley will no longer be called Topheth, but the Valley of Slaughter.

While the story is unique to Jeremiah and the specific context in which he lived, the message is still relevant today. It serves as a warning against the dangers of idolatry and the shedding of innocent blood and a reminder that God will not tolerate such wickedness forever. We should heed God's warning and turn away from sin, seeking forgiveness and righteousness through Jesus Christ.

Daniel stopped eating the king's food

But Daniel purposed in his heart that he would not defile himself with the portion of the king's delicacies, nor with the wine which he drank; therefore he requested of the chief of the eunuchs that he might not defile himself.

Now God had brought Daniel into the favor and goodwill of the chief of the eunuchs. And the chief of the eunuchs said to Daniel, "I fear my lord the king, who has appointed your food and drink. For why should he see your faces looking worse than the young men who are your age? Then you would endanger my head before the king." Daniel 1: 8-10

During the exile, Judah's most talented and intelligent young men were taken to Babylon's king's court. The king instructed that they be served the most exquisite food from his kitchens. However, Daniel refused to eat it, probably because he knew some had been offered to idols. So instead of consuming wine and rich meats, Daniel asked for vegetables and water.

Daniel's decision to abstain from the king's food was not just about following dietary laws, but also about remaining faithful to God in a foreign land. By refusing to eat the king's food, Daniel demonstrated his commitment to God and willingness to stand up for his beliefs, even in the face of potential consequences.

His decision ultimately led to God's favor, as he and his companions were healthier and more capable than the others who ate the king's food. This story teaches us the importance of staying true to our beliefs, even when difficult or unpopular, and trusting that God will bless our obedience.

The Consecrated Life of the Prophet

Then the Lord spoke to Moses, saying, "Speak to the children of Israel, and say to them: 'When either a man or woman consecrates an offering to take the vow of a Nazirite, to separate himself to the Lord, he shall separate himself from wine and similar drink; he shall drink neither vinegar made from wine nor vinegar made from similar drink; neither shall he drink any grape juice, nor eat fresh grapes or raisins.

All the days of his separation he shall eat nothing that is produced by the grapevine, from seed to skin. 'All the days of the vow of his separation no razor shall come upon his head; until the days are fulfilled for which he separated himself to the Lord, he shall be holy. Then he shall let the locks of the hair of his head grow.

All the days that he separates himself to the Lord he shall not go near a dead body. He shall not make himself unclean even for his father or his mother, for his brother or his sister, when they die, because his separation to God is on his head. All the days of his separation he shall be holy to the Lord. Numbers 6:2-8

The life of a prophet in the Old Testament strongly emphasizes the principle of consecration. This principle is rooted in the practice of the Nazarites, as prescribed in Numbers 6:2-8. The Nazarites were individuals who voluntarily separated themselves from the rest of society and consecrated themselves to God.

The vow of a Nazarite included abstaining from wine and strong drinks, not cutting their hair during the entire period of the vow, and avoiding contact with the dead.

Although there is no record of any Nazarites before Samson, it is evident that they existed even before Moses. Abraham and Joseph are two examples of individuals who lived as Nazarites. Likewise, the Old Testament prophets lived as people set apart unto God, and their lives were submitted to Him.

Only three individuals are mentioned in Scripture as being

Nazarites for life: Samson, Samuel, and John the Baptist. These unique appearances and commands were God's ways of speaking to the children of Israel. The Nazarite vow reminds us that a consecrated life involves sacrifice and separation from the world and that our lives belong to God.

The relationship between God and the Children of Israel in the Old Testament was unique and special. God communicated with His people in various ways, some of which may seem foreign today.

However, these practices were specific to the Children of Israel and not necessarily applicable to other nations. The Prophets and the Children of Israel understood and embraced these practices because they were the ways in which a great God communicated with them.

While practices were specific to that time in Israel's history, the principles that God established are eternal and unchanging. These principles are not subject to cultural contexts and should not be compromised or violated.

False Prophets

The presence of false prophets in the Old Testament is a critical consideration when examining the relationship between God and His people. These imposters claimed to be sent by God, but they were not. Instead, they often undermined the authentic prophets sent by God.

False prophets frequently delivered messages that contradicted the message of God's true prophets. They spoke falsely and led people astray from the truth. As a result, it was essential for the Israelites to distinguish between genuine and counterfeit prophets and to follow the true messengers of God.

The presence of false prophets also highlights the importance of testing every spirit to determine if it is from God, as instructed in the New Testament (1 John 4:1). Today, it remains crucial to discern between true and false teachings and prophets to avoid being misled.

Chapter 4

Prophetic Ministry in the New Testament

"The New Testament prophet is a messenger of God who brings a word that is both corrective and redemptive, pointing people back to God and His purposes for their lives." - A.W. Tozer

The New Testament is overflowing with stories of miracles, divine interventions, and teachings from Jesus and the apostles. Also nestled within these pages lies the New Testament prophetic ministry.

From the prophetic utterances of Jesus to the foretelling of his ultimate return, the prophets of the New Testament were key players in shaping the early Christian Church. In this chapter, we'll explore the fascinating world of the prophetic ministry in the New Testament and how it continues to impact our faith today.

As we have seen so far, throughout the Old Testament, God had a special covenant with Israel, and the prophets served as His primary mouthpiece to deliver His messages. These prophets were the chosen few who conveyed God's word to the masses. For centuries, this was the go-to method of communication between God and His people, all the way up until the arrival of John the Baptist.

The People of the New Testament

The dawn of the New Testament era brought a new and unique identity for God's people. Unlike the requirements and regulations placed upon Israel in the Old Testament, the people of the New Testament did not have to earn their salvation. They were no longer under the law but under grace.

This grace was manifested through Jesus Christ, who willingly took the weight of humanity's sins upon himself. Through his selfless sacrifice and unwavering obedience to God, the sins of Adam were utterly eradicated, and anyone who came to God with a simple faith in Jesus was granted righteousness in the eyes of the Lord.

This seismic shift in how God dealt with His people was a radical departure from the strict rules and rituals of the Old Testament. It opened the door for anyone and everyone to be welcomed into the fold of God's love, regardless of their background or circumstances.

In John 3:5-6, Jesus explains that being born of the Spirit is necessary to enter the kingdom of God.

> *Jesus answered, "Most assuredly, I say to you, unless one is born of water and the Spirit, he cannot enter the kingdom of God. That which is born of the flesh is flesh, and that which is born of the Spirit is spirit.*

This new birth, being born of the Spirit, is available to anyone who believes in Jesus Christ as their Lord and Savior, regardless of their previous lineage or circumstances. As John 1:12-13 states,

> *He was in the world, and the world was made through Him, and the world did not know Him. He came to His own, and His own did not receive Him. But as many as received Him, to them He gave the right to become children of God, to those who believe in His name: who were born, not of blood, nor of the will of the flesh, nor of the will of man, but of God.*

We see here that those who receive Jesus Christ are given the right to become children of God, born not of blood, nor of the will of the flesh, nor of the will of man, but of God. This emphasizes the idea that through Jesus Christ, all are welcome in the kingdom of God, and one's past or lineage does not hinder their access to salvation.

The ones who opened their hearts to receive God's grace became known as believers. The New Testament paints a beautiful picture of these believers assembled as the Church. Unlike the Old Testament, which emphasized circumcision, the New Testament tells us that true membership in the Church was determined by the circumcision of one's heart.

The beauty of the Church is eloquently expressed in 1 Corinthians 12:12-14, where Paul likens the Church to a single body made up of many different parts.

> *For as the body is one and has many members, but all the members of that one body, being many, are one body, so also is*

Christ. For by one Spirit we were all baptized into one body—whether Jews or Greeks, whether slaves or free—and have all been made to drink into one Spirit. For in fact the body is not one member but many.

Through the power of the Holy Spirit, believers of all races, tribes, and backgrounds are brought together and united in their shared faith in Christ.

This radical inclusivity was a hallmark of the early Christian Church, and it continues to resonate with believers around the world today. In a world that's often divided by borders and boundaries, the message of the New Testament Church serves as a powerful reminder of the unifying force of faith.

No matter who you are or where you come from, if you have faith in Christ, you are a vital and valued member of the Church, united with your fellow believers by the unbreakable bond of the Holy Spirit.

What are the People of God in the New Testament Called?

The New Testament is full of references to the people of God and the many names by which they are called. These names reflect the centrality of the Lord Jesus Christ in the family of God and emphasize believers' special relationship with Him. Let's explore a few of these names in more detail:

The Body of Christ. First and foremost, the people of God are referred to as the Body of Christ. This term is used in Ephesians 1:22-23, which describes Christ as the head of the Church, His body. This metaphor emphasizes the unity of believers, who are all connected to one another through their relationship with Christ. Like the various parts of a body, each believer has a unique role to play in the Church, but all work together to achieve a common goal.

The Church of the Living God. Another name used to describe the people of God is the Church of the Living God, as mentioned in 1 Timothy 3:15. This name highlights that God is alive and active in the world and that His people are a living testimony to His power and presence. Therefore, as members of the Church of the Living God, believers are responsible for behaving in a manner that reflects the truth and grace of God.

The General Assembly and the Firstborn is another name that the people of God are called in the New Testament. This name appears in Hebrews 12:22-23, which describes the heavenly city of Jerusalem and the countless angels surrounding it. This name emphasizes that believers are part of a larger community of faith that spans time and eternity.

Lamb's Bride. The people of God are also referred to as the Lamb's Bride in Revelation 21:9. This name emphasizes the intimate relationship that believers have with Christ, often called the Lamb of God. Just as a bride is united with her groom in marriage, so too are believers united with Christ intimately and meaningfully.

How God spoke to the people of the New Testament

God speaks through Jesus. The writer of Hebrews makes this clear in the opening verses of the book that God speaks to His people in the new covenant through His Son, Jesus Christ.

God, who at various times and in various ways spoke in time past to the fathers by the prophets,has in these last days spoken to us by His Son, whom He has appointed heir of all things, through whom also He made the worlds;

who being the brightness of His glory and the express image of His person, and upholding all things by the word of His power, when He had by Himself purged our sins, sat down at the right hand of the Majesty on high,

having become so much better than the angels, as He has by inheritance obtained a more excellent name than they. Hebrews 1:1-4

Jesus was not just a wise teacher. He was the very image of God, the brightness of His glory. God appointed Him as the heir of all things, and through Him, God made the world. Jesus was not just a messenger; he was the message. He was the embodiment of God's love and grace.

Throughout His life on earth, people looked up to Jesus. They brought the sick to Him to be healed and spent days sitting at His feet, listening to His words. Nicodemus, a religious leader of his day, came to Jesus at night to ask questions about the kingdom of God.

Mary, when Jesus came to Bethany after the death of her brother Lazarus, said, "If you had been here, my brother would not have died." This showed that people looked to Jesus for hope and salvation.

Jesus' disciples also looked to Him. They knew that without Him, they could do nothing. When Jesus told them that it was time for Him to go away, they were filled with sorrow. But Jesus reassured them that He was not leaving them as orphans.

Instead, he promised to send them the Holy Spirit, who would guide them and teach them all things.

In Jesus, God spoke to humanity in a way they could understand. He spoke to them through His life, teachings, miracles, and ultimately through His death, resurrection, and ascension. He showed them the love and grace of God in a way that had never been seen before. Jesus was the culmination of God's plan to redeem humanity and bring them back into a relationship with Him. Through Jesus, God spoke to humanity, and His message continues to speak to us today.

God speaks through the Holy Spirit. Jesus told His followers that He would never leave or forsake them. But the disciples realized Jesus' crucifixion and death were impending, so they were afraid and worried. But Jesus assured them that the Holy Spirit would come to them and never leave them.

It says in John 14:15-18:

> *If you love Me, keep My commandments. And I will pray the Father, and He will give you another Helper, that He may abide with you forever—the Spirit of truth, whom the world cannot receive, because it neither sees Him nor knows Him; but you know Him, for He dwells with you and will be in you. I will not leave you orphans; I will come to you.*

The Holy Spirit is the Spirit of truth, and through the Spirit, believers in Christ can understand and know God. The Holy Spirit is a seal, a mark of God's ownership, on those who belong to Him. The Spirit indwells the believer, filling them with power and instruction so that they can live according to God's commandments.

The Old Testament prophet Ezekiel also spoke of the Holy Spirit, writing about God's promise to give the believer a new heart and a new spirit.

For I will take you from among the nations, gather you out of all countries, and bring you into your own land. Then I will sprinkle clean water on you, and you shall be clean; I will cleanse you from all your filthiness and from all your idols. I will give you a new heart and put a new spirit within you; I will take the heart of stone out of your flesh and give you a heart of flesh. I will put My Spirit within you and cause you to walk in My statutes, and you will keep My judgments and do them. Ezekiel 36:24-27

God promised to give believers a new heart, which means a renewal of the human spirit to make it soft and receptive to His guidance. He also promised to put His Spirit within humans.

In Romans 8:13-16, we read:

For if you live according to the flesh you will die; but if by the Spirit you put to death the deeds of the body, you will live. For as many as are led by the Spirit of God, these are sons of God. For you did not receive the spirit of bondage again to fear, but you received the Spirit of adoption by whom we cry out, "Abba, Father." The Spirit Himself bears witness with our spirit that we are children of God...

The Holy Spirit empowers believers to live a life that glorifies God and to walk in His statutes. According to the Apostle

Paul, living according to the Spirit means putting to death the deeds of the flesh.

By following the Spirit, believers become the children of God, who can cry out to Him saying, "Abba, Father." The Holy Spirit is the seal of God that confirms believers' status as His children.

Therefore, the Holy Spirit is crucial in the believer's life as our helper, teacher, and guide. He empowers us to live according to the fruit of the Spirit and provides assurance that we are God's children. Through the Holy Spirit, God speaks to humanity, and we can live a life that glorifies Him.

God speaks through the human spirit. In the Book of Job, it is written that there is a spirit within man and that the Spirit of God instructs man through this spirit.

> So Elihu, the son of Barachel the Buzite, answered and said: "I am young in years, and you are very old; Therefore, I was afraid, and dared not declare my opinion to you. I said, 'Age should speak, and multitude of years should teach wisdom.' But there is a spirit in man, and the breath of the Almighty gives him under-standing. Great men are not always wise, nor do the aged always understand justice. Job 32: 6-9

This declaration in the book of Job underscores the critical role the human spirit plays in our connection with God, with the spirit being viewed as central and superior to the mind. In the book of Proverbs, King Solomon also acknowledges the importance of the human spirit: *The spirit of a man is the lamp of the Lord, Searching all the inner depths of his heart.* (Proverbs 20:27)

Through divine inspiration, King Solomon affirmed that the human spirit provides the mind with vital information for successful living on earth. As a Christian, your spirit is a crucial aspect of your experience with God as it enables you to receive directly from the Holy Spirit and convey this information to your soul, where your mind resides and operates.

In his writing, the Apostle John discusses the anointing believers receive when they come to Jesus and surrender their lives to Him.

> *Little children, it is the last hour; and as you have heard that the Antichrist is coming, even now many antichrists have come, by which we know that it is the last hour.*
>
> *They went out from us, but they were not of us; for if they had been of us, they would have continued with us; but they went out that they might be made manifest, that none of them were of us.*
>
> *But you have an anointing from the Holy One, and you know all things. I have not written to you because you do not know the truth, but because you know it, and that no lie is of the truth.* 1 John 2:18-21

Consider what the Apostle said about the state of man because of the anointing of the Holy Spirit. He asserts that you know all things because of it. This statement can be interpreted as both completed and continuous.

It is completed because God always declares the end from the beginning, but it is also continuous because God guides us through the process of becoming what He is working in us. You are currently in the process of gaining knowledge of everything

God wants you to know, which establishes the ongoing work of the anointing in your life.

If these passages still leave you with questions, consider the significant 1 John 2:26-27, where the Apostle elaborates further:

> These things I have written to you concerning those who try to deceive you. But the anointing which you have received from Him abides in you, and you do not need that anyone teach you; but as the same anointing teaches you concerning all things, and is true, and is not a lie, and just as it has taught you, you will abide in Him.

The Apostle John highlights the crucial role of sensitivity to the Holy Spirit. Our human spirit acts as a receiver of God's Spirit; without this ability, our lives lack meaning.

The profound truth conveyed here is that if you adopt listening to the Holy Spirit as a way of life, you will reach a stage where you no longer need to seek direction from any human.

However, the challenge is that people often fail to develop their spirits to a level where they can receive what the Holy Spirit communicates. This underdevelopment is responsible for the dependency syndrome among many Christians today.

Instead of relying on the Holy Spirit, they seek guidance from others who offer insights into their future. They move from place to place, seeking emotional experiences with prophets, but their spirits remain unfulfilled and undeveloped.

God speaks to us through New Testament Prophets. Although the New Testament, particularly the early Church, contains fewer examples of prophetic ministry compared to the Old Testament, it remains significant.

For example, the Book of Acts documents the prophetic ministry of Agabus, a prominent example in the New Testament.

> *And when we had finished our voyage from Tyre, we came to Ptolemais, greeted the brethren, and stayed with them one day. On the next day we who were Paul's companions departed and came to Caesarea, and entered the house of Philip the evangelist, who was one of the seven, and stayed with him.*
>
> *Now this man had four virgin daughters who prophesied. And as we stayed many days, a certain prophet named Agabus came down from Judea.*
>
> *When he had come to us, he took Paul's belt, bound his own hands and feet, and said, "Thus says the Holy Spirit, 'So shall the Jews at Jerusalem bind the man who owns this belt, and deliver him into the hands of the Gentiles.'"* Acts 21:7-10

It is noteworthy that in this passage, the prophesying of Philip's four daughters is mentioned, but the content of their prophecy remains unspecified.

However, upon Agabus' arrival, his prophetic authority is immediately recognized as he delivers a clear and unambiguous message about what will happen to Paul if he goes to Jerusalem.

Biblical scholars make a distinction between the gift of prophecy and the office of the prophet, with the latter involving collaboration with other spiritual gifts.

It is possible to possess the gift of prophecy without occupying the office of the prophet, and this is a crucial differentiation that is often overlooked. While Philip's daughters manifested the gift of prophecy, Agabus operated from the office of the prophet, which made a significant difference.

Agabus is mentioned again in the Book of Acts, where he prophesies about a coming famine in the world, which the writer later confirms happened during the reign of Claudius Caesar.

And in these days, prophets came from Jerusalem to Antioch. Then one of them, named Agabus, stood up and showed by the Spirit that there was going to be a great famine throughout all the world, which also happened in the days of Claudius Caesar. Then the disciples, each according to his ability, determined to send relief to the brethren dwelling in Judea. This they also did, and sent it to the elders by the hands of Barnabas and Saul. Acts 11:27-30

Agabus made two futuristic prophecies. One was about Apostle Paul, and the other was about a coming famine in the world.

Besides Agabus, the New Testament also makes references to other prophets. Here is one such instance in Acts 13:1-3:

Now in the Church that was at Antioch there were certain prophets and teachers: Barnabas, Simeon who was called Niger, Lucius of Cyrene, Manaen who had been brought up with Herod the tetrarch, and Saul.

As they ministered to the Lord and fasted, the Holy Spirit said, "Now separate to Me Barnabas and Saul for the work to which I have called them." Then, having fasted, prayed, and laid hands on them, they sent them away.

Notice the entire Church was gathered, and among them were prophets and teachers. The prophets spoke directionally about a missionary journey and gave guidance to the Church in fulfilling Jesus' command to spread the Gospel to the world.

Just as the Old Testament prophets called people back to Moses' words, the New Testament prophets referred back to the Great Commission given by Jesus. Understanding this distinction is essential in interpreting modern prophecies. It's crucial to ask where modern prophets are positioned in God's grand plan and what they aim to achieve.

The final narrative in the Book of Acts occurred when the Church came together, and prophets Judas and Silas exhorted and strengthened the brethren with many words. While the Bible did not provide the details of the exhortation, there was no indication that these words had a specific direction or futuristic implications.

Acts 15:30-32 reads:

So when they were sent off, they came to Antioch; and when they had gathered the multitude together, they delivered the letter. When they had read it, they rejoiced over its encouragement. Now Judas and Silas, themselves being prophets also, exhorted and strengthened the brethren with many words. And after they had stayed there for a time, they were sent back with greetings from the brethren to the apostles.

So, we can see that Judas and Silas were prophets who

exhorted and strengthened the brethren through their words. There was no indication of them making predictions or fore-telling the future. Instead, they were focused on forth-telling - speaking forth messages of encouragement and edification to the believers.

The Apostle Paul as a New Testament Prophet

The Apostle Paul is also recognized as a prominent prophet of the New Testament. His writings showcase both aspects of the work of the prophet.

First, he engages in forth-telling by offering practical instructions for living in light of the new covenant established by God through Jesus Christ. Paul's forth-telling covers a broad range of topics, including personal growth and development, relationships within the body of Christ, our response to current events and earthly authorities, handling finances, living a holy life, and acknowledging Jesus as Lord over all.

For example, in Colossians 3:12, we see how Paul operated in the prophetic office of forth-telling:

Therefore, as the elect of God, holy and beloved, put on tender mercies, kindness, humility, meekness, longsuffering; bearing with one another, and forgiving one another, if anyone has a complaint against another; even as Christ forgave you, so you also must do.

But above all these things put on love, which is the bond of perfection.

And let the peace of God rule in your hearts, to which also you were called in one body; and be thankful.

> *Let the word of Christ dwell in you richly in all wisdom, teaching and admonishing one another in psalms and hymns and spiritual songs, singing with grace in your hearts to the Lord.*
>
> *And whatever you do in word or deed, do all in the name of the Lord Jesus, giving thanks to God the Father through Him.*

Paul also spoke about future events, particularly on the Second coming of the Lord. He wrote extensively about what we are experiencing in these last days, as seen in his letters to Timothy and the Thessalonians.

He was focused on heaven and not this earth, urging believers to live in a way that reflects their eternal destiny and to eagerly anticipate the return of Christ. An example of this can be found in 1 Thessalonians 4:13-18:

> *But I do not want you to be ignorant, brethren, concerning those who have fallen asleep, lest you sorrow as others who have no hope. For if we believe that Jesus died and rose again, even so God will bring with Him those who sleep in Jesus.*
>
> *For this we say to you by the word of the Lord, that we who are alive and remain until the coming of the Lord will by no means precede those who are asleep.*
>
> *For the Lord Himself will descend from heaven with a shout, with the voice of an archangel, and with the trumpet of God. And the dead in Christ will rise first.*
>
> *Then we who are alive and remain shall be caught up together with them in the clouds to meet the Lord in the air. And thus we shall always be with the Lord. Therefore comfort one another with these words.*

The Vital Role of the Prophetic in the Early Church

The prophetic ministry in the New Testament played a vital role in the life of the early Church. The prophets were not just foretellers but also forth-tellers who spoke to the present situations and the spiritual well-being of the people. They provided direction, guidance, and correction to the Church, helping the believers to understand and apply the teachings of Christ.

The Apostle Paul is a prime example of a New Testament prophet whose writings guide us today. Therefore, the prophetic ministry is still relevant in the Church today. We should seek to discern the true prophets from the false ones, ensuring that the prophetic word is always aligned with the principles laid out for us in the New Testament.

Chapter 5

The Revelation Gifts

"The gift of prophecy is a powerful tool that the Holy Spirit has given to the Church. When it is in operation, it brings edification, exhortation, and comfort to the body of Christ." Kenneth Hagin

As believers in Christ, we are called to walk in the Spirit and live a life that is pleasing to God. One of the ways God helps us to walk in His will is through men and women of God ministering through the revelation gifts of the Spirit, which include the Word of knowledge, the Word of wisdom, and the discerning of spirits.

In this chapter, we will explore the nature of these gifts and how they operate in the life of a believer. We will examine the biblical basis for these gifts and their practical applications in our daily lives. We will also look at some common misconceptions about these gifts and how to avoid the pitfalls of misusing them.

Let's begin with 1 Corinthians 12:4-11:

There are diversities of gifts, but the same Spirit. There are differences of ministries, but the same Lord. And there are diversities of activities, but it is the same God who works all in all.

But the manifestation of the Spirit is given to each one for the profit of all: for to one is given the Word of wisdom through the Spirit, to another the Word of knowledge through the same Spirit, to another faith by the same Spirit, to another gifts of healings by the same Spirit, to another the working of miracles, to another prophecy, to another discerning of spirits, to another different kinds of tongues, to another the interpretation of tongues.

But one and the same Spirit works all these things, distributing to each one individually as He wills.

Word of Knowledge

The gift of the Word of Knowledge refers to the supernatural ability to know information about a situation or a spiritual principle that could not have been obtained naturally. This gift enables someone to perceive a situation as God sees it. The Word of Knowledge remains a crucial gift in the church today.

There are different ways this gift operates, including:

- Communicating divine revelation.
- Providing divine knowledge and insight into past and present circumstances.

The Word of Knowledge manifests when the Holy Spirit

reveals information to an individual about another person's condition. This gift does not always come with great pomp and circumstance and can even be exercised without the individual being aware of it.

In the gospel of John, we see an example of Jesus exercising the **gift of the Word of Knowledge with Nathanael**. Nathanael expressed surprise when Jesus greeted him, saying, "How do you know me?" (John 1:48).

In response, Jesus revealed that He had seen Nathanael before Philip called him and even knew where Nathanael had been at that time. Jesus had perceived Nathanael's presence under a fig tree, which Nathanael had not mentioned to anyone.

This revelation was beyond what could have been known naturally, indicating that Jesus had exercised the gift of the Word of Knowledge. He supernaturally knew the details of Nathanael's whereabouts and actions, providing evidence of His divinity and authority.

It was a sign to Nathanael that Jesus was the promised Messiah, the Son of God, and that He knew Nathanael's heart and character. Nathanael recognized this, exclaiming, *"Rabbi, You are the Son of God! You are the King of Israel!"* (John 1:49).

In John 4, we see another instance where Jesus exercised the gift of the **Word of Knowledge, this time with a Samaritan woman at a well**. When Jesus asked her to go and bring her husband, the woman replied that she had no husband.

However, Jesus knew this was not the whole truth and revealed to her that she had, in fact, had five husbands and was currently living with a man who was not her husband.

This revelation was beyond what could be known naturally,

indicating that Jesus had exercised the gift of the Word of Knowledge. He supernaturally knew the details of the woman's life and situation, providing evidence of His divinity and authority.

Furthermore, Jesus's use of the Word of Knowledge in this situation served a specific purpose. It was a sign to the woman that Jesus was the Messiah who knew all things and could offer her living water, the gift of eternal life.

The woman recognized this and declared to Jesus, "I know that Messiah is coming (He who is called Christ); when that One comes, He will declare all things to us" (John 4:25). Jesus responded, "I who speak to you am He" (John 4:26).

In Matthew 16:13-20, we find another instance where the gift of the Word of Knowledge was exercised, with **Simon Peter's confession of Jesus as the Messiah**.

First, Jesus asked his disciples, *"Who do people say that the Son of Man is?"* (Matthew 16:13). After the disciples offered various opinions, Jesus asked them directly, *"But who do you say that I am?"* (Matthew 16:15).

It was then that Simon Peter replied, *"You are the Christ, the Son of the living God"* (Matthew 16:16).

Jesus's response to Peter's confession was telling. He affirmed that this revelation did not come from Peter's natural understanding but from a supernatural source.

Jesus said to Peter, *"Blessed are you, Simon Bar-Jonah! For flesh and blood has not revealed this to you, but my Father who is in heaven"* (Matthew 16:17).

In this instance, the Word of Knowledge revealed Jesus's identity to Simon Peter. It was not something Peter could have deduced on his own but was a supernatural insight God gave him. This revelation was crucial in confirming Peter's faith and establishing his leadership role among the apostles.

Despite some arguments that the gift of the Word of Knowledge is no longer needed today, it is still a relevant and vital gift for the church. The gift can provide supernatural insight and understanding into various situations, aiding in the furtherance of the Christian ministry.

Word of Wisdom

The Holy Spirit's gift of wisdom is essential for believers to navigate through life in a way that honors God. This gift involves applying knowledge and insight in a practical way to everyday situations, enabling believers to align with God's will.

This gift allows believers to see life from God's perspective and make decisions based on His wisdom rather than their limited understanding. It transcends human genius and insight; only the Holy Spirit can impart this Word of Wisdom. As Paul wrote, "the foolishness of God is wiser than human wisdom" (1 Corinthians 1:25).

While all Christians are encouraged to seek wisdom through prayer and studying God's Word, the gift of the Word of Wisdom is a supernatural ability given by the Holy Spirit. It cannot be attained through human effort, knowledge, or experience.

The Word of Wisdom is different from the Word of Knowledge, another spiritual gift mentioned in 1 Corinthians 12:8. The Word of Knowledge involves a supernatural revelation of facts that enable us to more effectively minister to the needs of people, know and understand situations, circumstances, sickness, demonic influence, etc.

In contrast, the Word of wisdom provides prophetic insight, guidance, and counsel for people, events, or things that have not yet happened for their proper end: the furtherance of God's kingdom.

The wisdom of humanity, also known as academic analysis, focuses on the knowledge gained from observing events that have occurred over time.

Formal educational institutions specialize in this type of wisdom, and individuals become experts in humanistic thinking. While this type of wisdom is useful for guiding people to live well on Earth, it is limited in terms of spiritual truth and understanding.

This is why the Word of Wisdom is crucial - it is a supernatural gift from God that surpasses human understanding and provides solutions when applied. It is a type of wisdom that cannot be acquired through study or experience but can only be bestowed by the Holy Spirit.

While academic scholars may struggle to understand spiritual truth, the Word of Wisdom is a gift available to believers who are open, receptive, yielded and sensitive to His promptings. He gives gifts severally as He wills.

The Bible is full of examples of how the Word of Wisdom was used by various individuals in different circumstances.

In Genesis 41, Joseph, a Hebrew slave imprisoned in Egypt, was summoned to interpret Pharaoh's dream. Not only did he interpret the dream, but he also had a Word of Wisdom on preparing for the future famine that the dream had foretold.

He advised Pharaoh to store grain during the seven years of

plenty so there would be enough food to survive during the seven years of famine. This Word of Wisdom was not based on Joseph's experience or knowledge, but it was given to him by God and saved many lives.

In Acts 21:11, the prophet Agabus exemplified the remarkable gift of the word of wisdom by unveiling a future event that awaited the Apostle Paul. Taking Paul's girdle, Agabus bound his own hands and feet, proclaiming, *"Thus saith the Holy Ghost, So shall the Jews at Jerusalem bind the man that owneth this girdle, and shall deliver him into the hands of the Gentiles."*

This powerful demonstration of prophecy unveils the profound connection between the gift of the Word of Wisdom and its manifestation in the predictions foretold by Jesus Himself in Matthew 24. Through the gift of prophecy, these revelations of future events serve as tangible evidence of the Word of Wisdom operating in the prophetic realm.

It is crucial to discern that while the gift of the Word of Knowledge reveals insights and understanding pertaining to the past and present, the prophetic revelations concerning the future fall within the realm of the gift of the Word of Wisdom.

This wisdom saved the lives of the army, and they were able to defeat their enemies.

In all these examples, we see that the Word of Wisdom is not just a theoretical concept but a practical gift that we, as believers, can use to navigate difficult situations. It is a gift from God, not based on human wisdom or experience. The Word of Wisdom is supernatural and can bring practical and life-saving solutions.

From what has been discussed in this chapter so far, it is becoming clear that for the prophetic ministry in the New

Testament to be effective - that is, if we are to function perfectly as God's mouthpiece - we should be exercising both the Word of Knowledge and the Word of Wisdom in the office of the prophet.

The Gifts Used in Tandem

The gifts of the Word of Knowledge and the Word of Wisdom often work in tandem to provide supernatural insight and understanding to believers.

The Word of Knowledge involves receiving specific information from the Holy Spirit about a situation or circumstance beyond natural knowledge. This gift is meant to provide clarity and understanding about a particular case.

The Word of Wisdom, on the other hand, involves the supernatural ability to apply that knowledge practically and effectively. It goes beyond simply understanding what is happening to how to navigate the situation in a way that aligns with God's will.

When the gift of the Word of Knowledge works together with the gift of the Word of Wisdom, the believer is equipped with the knowledge and understanding of a situation and the practical insight to navigate it with wisdom.

This combination of gifts can be especially powerful in areas such as decision-making, leadership, and ministry.

For instance, a person may receive a Word of Knowledge about a particular individual's struggle, revealing their situation's root cause.

With this knowledge, the Holy Spirit can then give the gift of the Word of Wisdom to provide practical steps for helping the person overcome their challenge in a way that aligns with God's plan.

Gift of Discernment

Discernment is the ability to distinguish between what is of God and what is not. It is the Holy Spirit revealing to a person what is true, false, good, or evil.

Every believer has a measure of discernment, but the gift of discerning spirits is a specific manifestation of the Holy Spirit's gifts listed in 1 Corinthians 12:10-11:

> to another the working of miracles, to another prophecy, to another discerning of spirits, to another different kinds of tongues, to another the interpretation of tongues. But one and the same Spirit works all these things, distributing to each one individually as He wills.

The gift of discerning spirits is the ability to see beyond the natural and identify the spirits at work in a situation. This gift enables the believer to identify demonic spirits, false teachings, and false prophets. It is important to note that this gift is not the same as being judgmental or critical but rather a gift of revelation from God.

As God's mouthpiece, the prophet requires both general discernment and the gift of the discerning of spirits to function effectively. The gift of the discerning of spirits is particularly important in the prophetic ministry as it helps the prophet to discern the source of the message they receive.

Is it from God, the devil, or from their own thoughts? This

gift enables the prophet to speak with accuracy and authority, avoiding deception and false teachings.

Every born-again believer filled with the Holy Spirit and speaking in tongues has a measure of discernment, which grows as the believer matures in the Spirit.

However, the Bible also mentions the specific gift of discerning spirits in 1 Corinthians 12:10-11. Prophets have access to both general discernment and this gift, and to be effective prophets, they need to exercise both gifts along with the Word of Knowledge and the Word of Wisdom.

In addition to recognizing the Holy Spirit, those with the gift of discernment can also identify evil spirits, including demons and the devil. They can discern when an unclean or oppressive spirit is at work in a person's life, causing afflictions or hindrances. They can discern the source of spiritual attacks or influences on individuals or groups.

The word discern means to see. You cannot see Jesus, angels, or demons without the gift of the discerning of spirits.

Chapter 6

Beware of False Prophets

"Beware of false prophets, who come to you in sheep's clothing but inwardly are ravenous wolves." - Jesus Christ, Matthew 7:15

I n a world where people are searching for God's guidance and direction, there has been an unfortunate rise of false prophets. These individuals, who claim to have divine insight and connection to a God, have deceived and misled vulnerable people for their own gain.

It's time to shine a light on these dark works and expose the works of those who go around parading as prophets.

When false prophets emerge, some people are drawn to them, while others are pushed away from God. These individuals often turn to the many humanistic organizations and philanthropists working hard to meet the needs of people. Governments, native medicine practitioners are all playing their part.

While many of these groups are undoubtedly well-meaning, there is a critical difference between what they do and what the Church and followers of Jesus Christ do. These non-Christian organizations are not driven by the Great Commission as outlined in Matthew 28:18-20, and they lack the perspective of heaven (Phil. 1:23-24).

Jesus issues a solemn warning to us in Matthew 7, urging us to take heed and not be led astray by the ones who only practice good works but who do not know Him.

> *Not everyone who says to Me, 'Lord, Lord,' shall enter the kingdom of heaven, but he who does the will of My Father in heaven. Many will say to Me in that day, 'Lord, Lord, have we not prophesied in Your name, cast out demons in Your name, and done many wonders in Your name?' And then I will declare to them, 'I never knew you; depart from Me, you who practice lawlessness!'*

Instead, it is the responsibility of the Body of Christ to arise and meet the needs of humanity while conforming to Christian principles and concepts taught in the Holy Bible.

As Jesus said in Mark 8:36-37, what good is it to gain the whole world if you lose your soul? And as Paul taught in 1 Corinthians 2:1-2, it's not about eloquence or worldly wisdom, but rather about knowing Jesus Christ and Him crucified.

We must be mindful of where we place our trust and ensure that any work done to meet human needs is grounded in Christian principles and values. Only then can we be sure that we are truly doing God's work and helping those in need without compromising our faith.

This principle applies equally to prophetic ministry. The prophetic must be grounded in guiding people to accept Jesus Christ as their Lord and Savior and bringing them closer to His kingdom.

Regrettably, our generation has witnessed considerable deviations and abuses within the Church and among so-called spiritual individuals and fringe groups who claim to practice the gifts of the Holy Ghost without adhering to God's Word or proven Christian leadership.

Let us not forget that the two most significant gifts bestowed upon us by God are the Gift of His Son (The Word) (John 1:14; John 3:16) and the Gift of the Holy Spirit (Acts 2:38).

However, despite these gifts, we still witness emotionalism, exaggerations, prophetic words at variance with God's Word, and peculiar ceremonies and actions by emerging "wannabe" prophets.

In 1 Corinthians 2:2, the Apostle Paul wrote to the Corinthians, *"For I determined not to know anything among you except Jesus Christ and Him crucified."*

Unfortunately, this is not always the case in many prophetic circles today. A new wave of religious syncretism is infiltrating the Church, which refers to the fusion of various religious beliefs and practices.

Now we hear of boiling sand, catching and releasing doves, and midnight sea bathing, all in the name of seeking divine direction. And the endless list of potions and concoctions some followers consume. God's Word is often overlooked in a generation seeking quick fixes and easy answers.

Whenever greed and deception come together, a Ponzi scheme is born. Similarly, when unsuspecting signs-seeking churchgoers encounter false prophets, it leads to religious deception, delusion, and emptiness.

The dangerous assumption is that if a spiritual experience "worked" and felt right, it must be of the Holy Spirit. This is a massive trap. Let me clarify that there are three possible sources of spiritual experiences and manifestations:

- God speaking (Exodus 20:1; Jeremiah 1:11-12; Acts 9:5-6)
- The devil (Matthew 4:8-9; Acts 16:16-18; 2 Corinthians 11:3)
- The human spirit (John 10:5; Colossians 2:4, 8; 2 Peter 2:1-20)

Experiences of hearing the devil speak without realizing it always lead to various forms of disaster. Experiences of hearing God speak and obeying Him always lead to fruitfulness.

Our human spirit can either align with the prompting of the Holy Spirit or be swayed by external influences. When the Holy Spirit confirms within our spirit, we can be confident that we are on the right path and experiencing God's will for our lives.

However, when we rely solely on emotional experiences without discernment or submission to God's Word, we may be led astray and miss out on the fullness of God's plan for us.

It's essential to recognize that there is a worldly imitation and a demonic counterfeit for every spiritual gift. We should not accept that if something attracts people and appears effective, it's automatically acceptable, regardless of its source.

This approach focuses on gaining followers rather than

leading them to salvation and discipleship in Christ; thus neglecting the Great Commission's mandate. We must never forget that our experiences should be rooted in sound theology based on the Word of God (Psalm 119:89).

Jesus warned of false prophets in Matthew 7:15-20, cautioning that they may appear outwardly innocent like sheep but be inwardly dangerous as ravenous wolves.

He advised that one could identify them by their fruits, emphasizing that a good tree cannot bear bad fruit, nor can a bad tree bear good fruit. Any tree that fails to produce good fruit is cut down and thrown into the fire.

Jesus also warned in Matthew 24:24 that false christs and false prophets would arise and perform great signs and wonders to lead astray, if possible, even the elect.

These false prophets might perform supernatural acts that can be appealing to people. However, it takes spiritual discernment to distinguish between the work of the Spirit of God and other spirits.

Think of the experience of the Apostle Paul as recorded in the Book of Acts:

> *Now it happened, as we went to prayer, that a certain slave girl possessed with a spirit of divination met us, who brought her masters much profit by fortune-telling.*
>
> *This girl followed Paul and us, and cried out, saying, "These men are the servants of the Most High God, who proclaim to us the way of salvation." And this she did for many days.*
>
> *But Paul, greatly annoyed, turned and said to the spirit, "I command you in the name of Jesus Christ to come out of her." And he came out that very hour.*

> *But when her masters saw that their hope of profit was gone,*
> *they seized Paul and Silas and dragged them into the market-*
> *place to the authorities.* Acts 16:16-19

How could Paul have known, except by discernment, that the girl was operating under the influence of an evil spirit and not of God?

Today, we must ask ourselves how many individuals are being deceived by those who appear to be performing supernatural acts but are not of God. Our current state of confusion illustrates the incredible power of deception that Jesus warned us about. He cautioned that even the elect may be led astray by these individuals without intervention.

Paul expressly warns against deception in the last days in his letter to Timothy:

> *But know this, that in the last days perilous times will come: For*
> *men will be lovers of themselves, lovers of money, boasters,*
> *proud, blasphemers, disobedient to parents, unthankful, unholy,*
> *unloving, unforgiving, slanderers, without self-control, brutal,*
> *despisers of good, traitors, headstrong, haughty, lovers of pleasure*
> *rather than lovers of God, having a form of godliness but*
> *denying its power.*
>
> *And from such people turn away! For of this sort are those*
> *who creep into households and make captives of gullible women*
> *loaded down with sins, led away by various lusts, always*
> *learning and never able to come to the knowledge of the truth.* 2
> Timothy 3:1-7

Note the graphic presentation of Paul concerning false

teachers and prophets. Whereas Jesus gave a generic description, Paul goes on to be more detailed in expatiating what Jesus said.

A recent survey compiled numerous fault lines in the operation of the prophetic gift both within and outside the Church, including the following:

- Twisting the Scripture to meet a particular need.
- Serving adulterated Communion Wine with herbs to hypnotize the flock.
- Giving out Lotto numbers on Radio.
- Hire fake sick and healed members to give testimonies.
- Comb Social Media platforms for information on members of host churches.
- Cases of planting objects in church members' homes for spiritual protection.

Signs of False Prophets and Deceptive Schemes

There is evidence, based on testimonies of victims and observations by both Christians and non-Christians, that false prophets exist, and that believers must be watchful. The following are a few examples of the fruits of false prophets, as warned by Jesus Christ Himself and explained by the Apostle Paul.

False Doctrines:

- False prophets deceive people by preaching false doctrines, sometimes with vivid illustrations, to make their followers believe they possess greater knowledge and understanding of spiritual things.
- Adulterated communion is a deceptive scheme that some false prophets use to keep their followers hooked and dependent on them rather than fostering a personal relationship with the Holy Spirit.
- False prophets brainwash their followers to accept everything they say without doing their own research, unlike the Berean believers who searched the scriptures for themselves.

Deceptive Schemes:

- False prophets use live radio broadcasts to ask their associates to call in with false testimonies about their experience with the prophet's ministry. This tactic attracts more people to follow them.
- False prophets manipulate people by staging fake healing and other miracles to deceive their followers.
- False prophets deploy the services of familiar spirits and use spiritual manipulation to bewitch people in order to exploit them. They produce false miracles to attract large crowds to their meetings and social media platforms.
- False prophets scour social media platforms for personal information on individuals and use it to

gain their attention and attract them to their ministry.

The Fear-Panic Syndrome

- False prophets create panic in the minds and hearts of people by prophesying pending doom and presenting themselves as having the power to set their victims free from the pending dangers.
- They send people to plant voodoo items and other fetish charms on people's property, including offices, churches, and homes, and then come themselves to locate it with prayer and incantations to extort money from their victims.
- They divide families by telling people that family members are causing them not to prosper in this life and offer solutions that make the people perpetually hooked on them.
- They threaten people with death and panic in the name of spiritual direction. This consists of devastating predictions, with the prophet having the power to deal with the predictions. By this, they get people to follow them perpetually, a never-ending cycle of "spiritual direction" to keep the exploitation going.

Extortion of Money

- False prophets ask people who have challenges and difficulties to pay large sums of money before seeing them for direction and end up worsening their problems because those directions do not come from God.

- They open their doors for counseling for a fee and use the information to prophesy openly in their meetings as if God had spoken to them.
- One such extortion scheme is the claim by false prophets that they can give you favor in whatever you do to double your money while you sit idling about. So, they ask people to pay money into certain accounts for the return of double. They initially pay a small amount into their victims' accounts and later dupe them.

Immoral Practices

For the prophecy came not in old time by the will of man: but holy men of God spake as they were moved by the Holy Ghost. 2 Peter 1:21

- They deceive emotionally vulnerable women by claiming that God wants them to perform a ritualistic bath, which often leads to sexual encounters.
- Despite the supposed anointing, these women's problems are not solved and are left worse off.

Self-Exaltation

False prophets spend more time talking about themselves and what God is doing through them rather than preaching the

Word. This self-promotion is used to manipulate ignorant and power-hungry followers.

Daniel did not take the credit for interpreting Nebuchadnezzar's dreams. He gave the glory to the Lord as described in Daniel 2:23:

> *I thank thee, and praise thee, O thou God of my fathers, who hast given me wisdom and might, and hast made known unto me now what we desired of thee: for thou hast now made known unto us the king's matter.*

False prophets have damaged people's confidence in the prophetic ministry and have tarnished its sanctity. While some may be skeptical of all prophets and their motives, it is essential to recognize that God still communicates through His servants.

Therefore, we must not allow false prophets to deceive people and rob them of the genuine prophetic ministry from God.

Chapter 7

How To Prepare Your Heart For the Prophetic Ministry

"If you want God to speak to you, make sure to spend more time in His Word than on the world's social media." - Beth Moore

There's nothing quite like the experience of hearing directly from God through His chosen vessels. It's a powerful moment where heaven meets earth, and God's voice is heard in a way that transforms lives, brings healing, and provides direction to believers through the prophetic word.

However, the question remains for many: how can you position yourself to receive the fullness of what God has in store for you? How can you prepare your heart to receive the prophetic ministry?

The answer lies in understanding the importance of spiritual preparation and being intentional about creating a space for God to speak to you through His prophets. In this chapter, we'll explore practical steps you can take to prepare your heart to receive the prophetic ministry and position yourself to experience the fullness of God's plan for your life.

Mindsets Undermining the Prophetic

As Christians, we are called to live according to God's Word and to uphold His values and teachings. But in this modern age, we are constantly bombarded by secular and liberal mindsets that seek to undermine our faith and lead us away from the truth.

These mindsets can infiltrate every aspect of our lives, including our churches and pulpits. That's why it's essential to recognize and address these 13 modern mindsets against Christ's Word.

The first mindset listed is egotism, characterized by believing that one can do whatever one wants without considering the consequences. This starkly contrasts what is taught in Romans 14:12, which reminds us that we will all give an account of ourselves to God.

The second mindset is emotion-based decision-making, which can lead us away from the truth of Christ's Word. Our feelings can deceive us and lead us to sin, as seen in Hebrews 5:14

The third mindset is innocence, where a person claims ignorance of what is wrong. However, Romans 12:1-3 teaches us to renew our minds and align them with God's Word.

The fourth mindset is conscience, where people may justify their actions because their conscience does not bother them. However, we are called to have a clear conscience before God

(Acts 24:16.) To have a clear conscience relates to our communication with people. In 1 Peter 3:15-16, it says,

> But in your hearts revere Christ as Lord. Always be prepared to give an answer to everyone who asks you to give the reason for the hope that you have. But do this with gentleness and respect, keeping a clear conscience so that those who speak maliciously against your good behavior in Christ may be ashamed of their slander.

This verse emphasizes the importance of being prepared to give a respectful and gentle answer to others about the reason for our hope in Christ, while maintaining a clear conscience.

The fifth mindset is rationality, where people may justify their actions based on what they perceive as harmless. However, Jesus teaches us in Matthew 22:26-40 to love God and our neighbor as ourselves and that all the law and prophets hang on these two commandments.

The sixth mindset is intuition, where a person may feel something is right even if it goes against biblical principles. However, we are called to abide in Christ's Word to know the truth, as seen in John 8:31-32.

The seventh mindset is hedonism, where people may prioritize their own pleasure above all else. However, Ephesians 5:18-19 teaches us to be filled with the Spirit, singing psalms and hymns, and making melodies in our hearts to the Lord.

The eighth mindset is statistics, where people may justify their actions because "everyone is doing it." However, we are called to be separate from the world and its ways, as seen in 1 John 2:15-17 and Colossians 1:13.

The ninth mindset is individualism, where a person may believe they are the master of their own fate. However, as believers, we are called to honor God with our bodies because they are temples of the Holy Spirit, as seen in 1 Corinthians 6:19-20.

The tenth mindset is relativism, where a person may believe that what they think is true if they believe it sincerely. However, we are called to put on the new self, created after the likeness of God in true righteousness and holiness, as seen in Ephesians 4:22-24 and Proverbs 3:5-6.

The eleventh mindset is consequence, where a person may believe that their actions do not harm anyone but themselves. However, we are called to consider others as more significant than ourselves, as seen in 2 Samuel 2:14 and Philippians 2:3-8.

The twelfth mindset is motivation, where people may justify their actions because they believe God knows their hearts. However, we are called to examine our hearts and confess our sins, as seen in Jeremiah 17:9-10 and Mark 7:20-23.

The thirteenth and final mindset is materialism, where a person may prioritize obtaining wealth by any means necessary. However, Jesus teaches us in Matthew 6:19-20 to forgive others as we have been forgiven and to prioritize eternal treasures over earthly ones.

These 13 modern mindsets can disadvantage the believer significantly when embracing the prophetic ministry. They have the potential to mislead us. Any believer consumed by these mindsets is not adequately prepared for a meaningful experience of the prophetic.

Cultivate the Right Mindset

To fully embrace the prophetic ministry, believers must cultivate mindsets prioritizing obedience to God's Word and submission to His will above their desires and worldly influences. They must be willing to examine their beliefs and behaviors, identify any areas of misalignment with God's Word, and seek repentance and transformation through the power of the Holy Spirit.

Develop your Spiritual life. The critical preparation for any believer to be ready for the prophetic ministry is to prioritize developing their spiritual life. This begins with being born again, receiving the indwelling of the Holy Spirit, and the assembling of the saints by joining a Bible believing church. However, while attending church, listening to sermons, and participating in programs is essential, it is not sufficient. True spiritual growth requires actively allowing the Word of God to transform you from the inside out.

Unfortunately, many Christians today have stopped short of genuinely developing their spiritual lives. While they may have overcome more commonly criticized sinful behaviors like fornication and stealing, they have not pursued deeper growth. As a result, their spirits remain stagnant, unable to hear the voice of the Holy Spirit even when He speaks loudly.

Each believer is responsible for cultivating and developing their human spirit, as the Bible calls for spiritual growth. When we neglect this aspect of our lives, we become lazy and dependent on others for spiritual sustenance. We become more susceptible to manipulation and deception from false prophets.

Don't let this be you. Instead, make it a priority to continually develop your spiritual life and grow closer to God. Only then can you be truly ready to receive and engage with the prophetic ministry.

Feed your spirit with the Word of God. Just like you nourish your physical body with a nutritious and balanced diet, your spirit thrives on the Word of God. Neglecting to read and study the Word of God will inevitably make your spirit dull, inactive, and unresponsive to the Holy Spirit's promptings. The Holy Spirit works in conjunction with the Word, so without the Word of God in your life, you cannot develop your spirit.

As you delve into the Scriptures, allow your mind to be renewed by the Word. You no longer live by your own opinions but submit every viewpoint to the scrutiny of God's Word. Any idea that contradicts the Word of God must be abandoned immediately and replaced by thoughts that align with Scripture. This is how true transformation occurs.

Exercise your spirit through prayer. The frequency and quality of your connection with God through prayer directly affect your spiritual alertness. Believers who spend more time in the presence of God are more likely to develop their spiritual man than those who do not. This is where praying in tongues becomes an advantage for believers who have experienced the baptism of the Holy Spirit. When you pray in tongues, your spirit communicates with God in mysteries your mind cannot comprehend. In the process, you are also strengthening your spirit.

Reflecting on how long you typically spend in prayer each day is essential. The duration of prayer in your private space is critical. But, apart from the duration, the quality of the time spent is equally important. Someone may spend an hour in prayer and have more fruitful fellowship with God than another who spends three hours. Allow the Holy Spirit to guide you and help you maximize your prayer time.

Develop sensitivity to the Holy Spirit. Sensitivity to the Holy Spirit is the most significant evidence of a fully developed spirit. As Christians, we are led by the Holy Spirit, not just by prophets, dreams, or prophesies. Therefore, developing sensitivity to His leading is essential for our growth in the Lord. Through prayer and Bible study, we can cultivate a deep relationship with God and increase our sensitivity to His voice. This sensitivity enables us to discern His will and follow His leading in all areas of our lives.

Praying in tongues is vital in developing sensitivity to the Holy Spirit. As we pray in tongues, our spirit is quickened, and we become more attuned to the Holy Spirit's leading. However, being sensitive to the Holy Spirit is not limited to our prayer time. It is a continuous practice that should permeate every aspect of our lives.

To be sensitive to the Holy Spirit, we must be open and receptive to His promptings. We should be willing to obey Him, even when it goes against our natural inclinations. This means we need to be intentional about listening to Him and seeking His guidance in everything we do. By doing so, we can experience a deeper, more fulfilling relationship with God and grow in our faith.

Believe not every spirit. The Apostle John exhorts us in the First Epistle of John, urging us to test the spirits and discern between those that come from God and those that do not. This message is conveyed in chapter 4, verses 1 through 4 of the letter.

Beloved, do not believe every spirit, but test the spirits, whether they are of God; because many false prophets have gone out into the world. By this you know the Spirit of God:

Every spirit that confesses that Jesus Christ has come in the flesh is of God and every spirit that does not confess that Jesus Christ has come in the flesh is not of God. And this is the spirit of the Antichrist, which you have heard was coming, and is now already in the world. 1 John 4:1-4

One of the benefits of a developed human spirit is the ability to discern spiritual activity around you. Every day, believers encounter the outpouring of the Spirit of God and the works of the devil.

That is why the Apostle warns us not to believe every spirit but to test them. The basis for testing spirits is the Word of God. Every true spirit honors the Lord Jesus Christ, so if Jesus is not honored in a place, it is best to leave before being affected by the negative spiritual activity.

Unfortunately, many people today rely on others to make decisions for them. For example, some are told which country to travel to or are promised visas and promotions in their work-place through false prophets.

Some even wait for a prophet to tell them whom to marry and break off relationships that could have blossomed into happy marriages. This dependency on others is the domination of man by man and prevents individuals from exercising their own discernment and developing their spiritual sensitivity.

Setting your life Apart - The life of Nazarites. As

a Christian, you are called to be a peculiar person, set apart from the world and dedicated to serving God.

It means living a life of Nazarites, just as Samson and John the Baptist did. It's a life of consecration, where you separate yourself from worldly desires and devote yourself entirely to God.

The passage in 1 Peter 2:9-10 tells us:

But you are a chosen generation, a royal priesthood, a holy nation, His own special people, that you may proclaim the praises of Him who called you out of darkness into His marvelous light; who once were not a people but are now the people of God, who had not obtained mercy but now have obtained mercy.

Hear what the Apostle Peter reminds us. We are a chosen generation, a holy nation, and a people of God's possession. Our purpose is to proclaim the praises of Him, who called us out of darkness and into His marvelous light. We have been saved by God's mercy, so we must live a life that reflects this mercy and grace.

It's also important to remember that our actions as Christians must always align with the revelations of Scripture. We cannot rely solely on our experiences or the experiences of others to guide our theology.

This is exemplified in 1 Samuel 10:1-7 and Acts 16:16-18, where we see how the actions of the Spirit agree with the revelations of Scripture.

We must, therefore, be careful not to build our theology solely on experiences but rather let our experiences be shaped by our understanding of God's Word.

We must always be grounded in the truth of Scripture and allow it to shape our beliefs and actions. This is emphasized in passages like Deuteronomy 18:22, 1 Samuel 3:19, and Matthew 24:35.

Living a life of Nazarites requires intentional dedication to God, and it's not always easy. However, with the help of the Holy Spirit and a commitment to following the truth of God's Word, we can live a life that is pleasing to Him and reflects His love and mercy to the world.

Be careful what you hear. Jesus warned us to be mindful of what we hear, saying, "If anyone has ears to hear, let him hear" (Mark 4:23). He further admonished us to "Take heed what you hear" (Mark 4:24) because daily news and reports can have an impact on our spirit.

Listening to negative or harmful information can corrupt our spirit, making it difficult to hear what the Holy Spirit says. Therefore, we must be mindful of what we allow to enter our minds and hearts, guarding ourselves against negative influences and prioritizing things that promote spiritual growth.

False news and incorrect teachings can undermine the fabric of our spiritual life and harm other areas of our lives. So instead, we should focus on hearing worthwhile things.

One effective way to achieve this is by getting a Bible app on our phones and listening to it when we are alone. This will help us to fill our minds with the truth of God's Word and remain sensitive to the leading of the Holy Spirit.

So beloved, remember that the prophetic ministry is a vital channel through which God speaks to His people. However, it requires the proper disposition of heart to receive the fullness of what God has in store for you.

By seeking after God through prayer, fasting, and studying His Word, you position yourself to receive the prophetic ministry in its fullness. You will be amazed at how God can transform your life and give you the direction and guidance you need to fulfill His purpose for your life.

Chapter 8

A Word for the True Modern-Day Prophet

"True prophets always point people to God, not to themselves."
- Mike Bickle

As the world continues to spin and new challenges arise, there are those among us who have been gifted with a unique ability to see beyond the veil of the mundane and into the realm of God. These modern-day prophets carry within them a sacred calling to speak the truth and bring hope to a world in desperate need.

But in a time when anyone can claim to be a prophet, it can be difficult to discern who is genuine and who is not. That's why, in this chapter, we will delve into the characteristics of the true modern-day Prophet, those who have been called by God to serve and are guided by a deep and abiding faith.

It's not enough to simply have a good heart or a desire to serve God. To be a prophet is to take on a weighty responsibility that requires a willingness to speak truth to power and challenge those who seek to deceive or mislead.

Despite the challenges that come with this sacred calling, the ministry of the prophet remains one of the most vital and impactful in our world today. The words and actions of true modern-day prophets can inspire and uplift, bring light to darkness, and hope to the hopeless.

So, I offer my gratitude and admiration to all the true modern-day prophets out there. You are a beacon of light in a world that so often seems lost in darkness, and your words and actions have the power to change lives and transform our world. In the following pages, I hope to offer insights and guidance that will help you fulfill your sacred calling and continue to be a force for good in our world.

Word of Knowledge and Word of Wisdom

The New Testament prophet's ministry relies heavily on two spiritual gifts highlighted in Paul's letter to the Corinthians (1 Corinthians 12) - the Word of Knowledge and the Word of Wisdom.

In today's prophetic meetings, we often witness an overemphasis on the gift of the Word of Knowledge, with little attention given to the gift of the Word of Wisdom. For instance, let's consider Johnnie's experience. During a prophetic gathering, a prophet told Johnnie that a promotion was in store for him, and within 30 days, his boss would offer him the new position. The crowd erupted in excitement and agreement.

True to the Prophet's words, Johnnie received the promotion. He excitedly shared his testimony on social media, further validating the Prophet's accuracy. However, six months later, Johnnie's new position turned out to be a liability, with several complaints against him for harassing his subordinates and behaving inappropriately with female colleagues.

Johnnie received a Word from the Prophet, but lacked the critical component of the Word of Wisdom, which reveals future events and would have forewarned and cautioned him to handle the new role with Godly character and integrity.

While the Word of Knowledge is a powerful gift that provides insight and revelation into past and present situations, the Word of Wisdom which gives you "advance knowledge" and reveals future outcomes and events, is often required to ensure that we apply the knowledge we receive in a way that aligns with God's will and serves His purpose.

Understand the Purpose of the Gift

As I pray for all true prophets, I desire that they grasp the purpose behind their calling and gift. The prophetic is not a means to accumulate wealth or achieve worldly success. It is not a tool to elevate oneself above others, nor is it intended to make people solely reliant on the Prophet's words.

My concern is with the trend of prophetic ministers gaining popularity through testimonies of people receiving financial, economic, and social blessings after partnering with them in ministry.

While such testimonies are encouraging, they can also create a competitive mindset among prophets, who may compete over whose prayers and declarations produce the greatest results.

This attitude can be harmful, leading to a lack of collaboration and division within the prophetic community. To prevent this, I turn to the Apostle Paul's teachings on spiritual gifts in the body of Christ, particularly in Ephesians, where he reminds us that each gift is essential and serves a unique purpose in building up the church.

> But to each one of us grace was given according to the measure of Christ's gift. Therefore He says: "When He ascended on high, He led captivity captive, and gave gifts to men." (Now this, "He ascended"—what does it mean but that He also first descended into the lower parts of the earth? He who descended is also the One who ascended far above all the heavens, that He might fill all things.)
>
> And He Himself gave some to be apostles, some prophets, some evangelists, and some pastors and teachers, for the equipping of the saints for the work of ministry, for the edifying of the body of Christ, till we all come to the unity of the faith and of the knowledge of the Son of God, to a perfect man, to the measure of the stature of the fullness of Christ;
>
> that we should no longer be children, tossed to and fro and carried about with every wind of doctrine, by the trickery of men, in the cunning craftiness of deceitful plotting,
>
> but, speaking the truth in love, may grow up in all things into Him who is the head—Christ— from whom the whole body, joined and knit together by what every joint supplies, according to the effective working by which every part does its share, causes growth of the body for the edifying of itself in love. Ephesians 4:7-16

God did not leave it to us to guess the purpose for the ministry gifts. The gifts were not given for the sake of those who manifest them, but for the growth of the body of Christ. They are intended to help every member of the body develop their spiritual life in all dimensions.

As Paul states 1 Corinthians 12:7, *"But the manifestation of the Spirit is given to every man to profit withal. A tree does not eat its own fruit. A tree bears fruit for others to eat."*

Only spiritually mature individuals will be able to withstand the winds of false doctrine and show in their lives the fullness of the measure of the stature of Christ. Such individuals will not elevate one prophet above the other, which can lead to unhealthy competition and eventual division in the body.

Self-Test

Let us apply a self-test to gauge the effectiveness of the ministry as prophets. Have you ever stopped to ponder over the following questions?

1.   How many people who call and share testimonies of what your prayers and declarations have done for them have expressed personal growth by simply following your ministry?

2.   How many people who got visas to travel internationally through your ministry serve God faithfully wherever they are?

3.   How many people following your ministry testify that they are experiencing transformation in their lives and are becoming better Christians than before encountering you?

We must ask ourselves these questions instead of waiting for God to ask us when we appear before Him one day to give an account of our ministry. We must understand that the fact that people are receiving material things does not necessarily mean they are growing spiritually. We can learn from the Hebrews who left Egypt under the leadership of Moses; they witnessed miracles, but almost all of them died in the wilderness because God was not pleased with them.

When we stand before God one day, He will judge us by Ephesians 4 and ask how many of the things He made Paul write there are found in our ministry. It will not be about how many prayer requests came to us and what we did with them.

"Believe my Prophets?"

What about the scripture that says, "believe in my prophets"?

> So they rose early in the morning and went out into the Wilderness of Tekoa; and as they went out, Jehoshaphat stood and said, "Hear me, O Judah and you inhabitants of Jerusalem: Believe in the Lord your God, and you shall be established; believe His prophets, and you shall prosper." 2 Chronicles 20:20

It is important to note that this statement was made under the Old Testament, where the Prophet was predominantly God's mouthpiece to the people. However, in the New Testament, we see a different modus operandi. The Prophet is not the mediator between God and man, but Jesus Christ is the mediator.

As it is written in 1 Timothy 2:5, "For there is one God and one mediator between God and mankind, the man Christ Jesus."

Therefore, in the New Testament, we are to believe in the

Lord Jesus Christ and follow His teachings, which are further clearly outlined in Hebrews 1:1-3:

> *God, who at various times and in various ways spoke in time*
> *past to the fathers by the prophets, has in these last days spoken*
> *to us by His Son, whom He has appointed heir of all things,*
> *through whom also He made the worlds;*
>
> > *who being the brightness of His glory and the express image*
> > *of His person, and upholding all things by the word of His*
> > *power, when He had by Himself purged our sins, sat down at the*
> > *right hand of the Majesty on high, having become so much better*
> > *than the angels, as He has by inheritance obtained a more excel-*
> > *lent name than they.*

This scripture in Hebrews means that Jesus is superior to all Prophets. God has chosen His Son Jesus as the mediator between God and humanity. No prophet could lay claim to such a declaration.

In John 1: 50-51, Jesus affirms that he greater than the prophets. He was the ladder Jacob saw in his dream in Genesis.

> *Jesus answered and said to him, "Because I said to you, 'I saw*
> *you under the fig tree,' do you believe? You will see greater*
> *things than these." And He said to him, "Most assuredly, I say to*
> *you, hereafter you shall see heaven open, and the angels of God*
> *ascending and descending upon the Son of Man."*

In talking with the people, Jesus said several times, "you have heard it said of old." The importance of that statement is that a new order is on board now. Let's see how Jesus explains the new order.

> "You have heard that it was said to those of old, 'You shall not murder, and whoever murders will be in danger of the judgment.' But I say to you that whoever is angry with his brother without a cause shall be in danger of the judgment.
>
> And whoever says to his brother, 'Raca!' shall be in danger of the council. But whoever says, 'You fool!' shall be in danger of hell fire.
>
> Therefore if you bring your gift to the altar, and there remember that your brother has something against you, leave your gift there before the altar, and go your way. First be reconciled to your brother, and then come and offer your gift. Matthew 5:21-24

And then later in the same chapter, Jesus adds:

> "You have heard that it was said, 'An eye for an eye and a tooth for a tooth.' But I tell you not to resist an evil person. But whoever slaps you on your right cheek, turn the other to him also.
>
> If anyone wants to sue you and take away your tunic, let him have your cloak also. And whoever compels you to go one mile, go with him two. Give to him who asks you, and from him who wants to borrow from you do not turn away. Matthew 5:38-42

Jesus brought a new level of clarity to the ancient words of the Prophets, infusing them with a deeper sense of purpose and meaning. His teachings shed light on the rationale behind many of the laws, revealing their true intentions.

Rather than seeking to abolish the law, Jesus came to fulfill it, to achieve what was once thought impossible: restoring humanity to God in a permanent and unbreakable bond.

Through his teachings and actions, Jesus guided mankind towards a closer relationship with the Holy Spirit, who resides within every believer. Even before the Day of Pentecost, he spoke about the vital role of the Spirit in the life of a believer, urging his followers to look to Him for guidance and strength. Jesus said:

"These things I have spoken to you while being present with you. But the Helper, the Holy Spirit, whom the Father will send in My name, He will teach you all things, and bring to your remembrance all things that I said to you." John 14:25-26

Since the dawn of time, God has desired that humanity looks to Him alone for their sustenance and purpose. Yet, over time, we have strayed from this divine pattern, seeking fulfillment, and meaning in worldly pursuits rather than in Him.

As a prophet of God, it is vital to avoid promoting anything against God's plan as revealed in Jesus Christ. If a prophet's followers begin to exalt the Prophet's name above that of Jesus, it is a dangerous path that leads to trouble and, ultimately, separation from God.

Jesus himself warned against the dangers of seeking approval from men, rather than from God, as what is highly esteemed among men is an abomination in the sight of God. He said in Luke 16:14-15:

Now the Pharisees, who were lovers of money, also heard all these things, and they derided Him. And He said to them, "You are those who justify yourselves before men, but God knows your hearts. For what is highly esteemed among men is an abomination in the sight of God.

When people begin to give more testimony to the Prophet than to Jesus, it is a time for caution, as it can be a sign of trouble brewing. It is far better to let the guidance of Ephesians 4 shape one's ministry and to focus on exalting the Holy Spirit in the hearts of men, rather than oneself.

The Apostle Paul advocated for a ministry that would bless believers and non-believers alike. He believed that if the prophets in the church spoke a word that revealed the secrets of the unbelievers' hearts, it would lead them to fall down and worship God.

Such revelations fall under the categories of the Word of Knowledge or the Word of Wisdom and may contain warnings, directions, or clarity about a particular situation.

However, due to the nature of these revelations, which often carry unique insights and information, they have often been misused and abused in the gatherings of the saints today, as pointed out by Apostle Paul in 1 Corinthians 14:23-25.

Therefore if the whole church comes together in one place, and all speak with tongues, and there come in those who are uninformed or unbelievers, will they not say that you are out of your mind?

But if all prophesy, and an unbeliever or an uninformed

person comes in, he is convinced by all, he is convicted by all. And thus the secrets of his heart are revealed; and so, falling down on his face, he will worship God and report that God is truly among you.

Therefore, it is essential to exercise caution and wisdom when handling such revelations, always remembering that they are meant to bring glory to God, not to the Prophet or anyone else.

Gradually Moving Away from Symbols

The prophetic ministry under the Old Testament vastly differed from what we see in the New Testament. One of the most significant changes was the move away from physical objects and symbols. In the Old Testament, physical symbols were used to represent shadows, but in the New Testament, the focus is on the real revelation of God - Jesus.

While physical symbols may help to strengthen one's faith to a certain level, they cannot sustain a believer in the long run. Faith rooted in symbols is an Old Testament fashion and must give way to a deeper, more personal faith in God's word.

As we make this shift, it is essential to have a humble learning attitude and understand the significance of this change. So here are a few shadows that must give way to the real as we move gradually away from symbols in our faith journey.

Anointing Oil - The Old Testament is replete with the use of anointing oil for various purposes, such as consecrating people and objects for particular tasks. However, a shift occurred with the advent of the New Testament and the ultimate sacrifice of Jesus Christ.

In Luke 4:16-18, Jesus declared that He was anointed by the Holy Spirit to proclaim the good news, free the captives, and bring sight to the blind. This anointing was not through physical oil but rather a spiritual impartation.

Jesus declared in Luke 4:16-18

He went to Nazareth, where he had been brought up, and on the Sabbath day he went into the synagogue, as was his custom. He stood up to read, and the scroll of the Prophet Isaiah was handed to him. Unrolling it, he found the place where it is written:

"The Spirit of the Lord is on me, because he has anointed me to proclaim good news to the poor. He has sent me to proclaim freedom for the prisoners and recovery of sight for the blind, to set the oppressed free, to proclaim the year of the Lord's favor."

This does not mean we cannot use anointing oil. But our faith must not be in the physical oil; neither should we use the oil in a "common" way to anoint anything and everything. Our faith must stand in the name of Jesus, the Word of God, and the Holy Spirit as we exercise the spiritual disciplines of prayer with fasting more than in physical symbols.

On the Day of Pentecost, the disciples received the same anointing without needing physical oil. Jesus never instructed that the anointing of the Holy Spirit should be accompanied by the use of anointing oil. While the use of physical objects can be beneficial, it is not necessary for experiencing the power and presence of God in one's life.

While some New Testament verses mention the use of

anointing oil, such as the book of James calling for the sick to be anointed with oil, it is not necessary for prayer to work and the power of God to be released.

Many people emphasize using physical symbols, such as anointing oil and holy water, to solicit God's mercy and favor. However, the true evidence of the anointing in our lives is the presence of the Holy Spirit within us. Our words and actions testify to God's power and grace as we obey Him.

While using anointing oil may not be sinful, relying too heavily on these physical symbols can limit our faith and hinder our spiritual growth. Instead, we should focus on building a deep, abiding relationship with God, walking in obedience to Him, and allowing His power to flow through us by building our faith in the scriptures and the Word of God.

Questioning the faith of those who rely solely on physical symbols rather than God Himself is vital. Are they genuinely trusting in God's power and mercy, or are they placing their faith in the symbols themselves? Ultimately, our faith should be firmly grounded in God's Word and the presence of His Holy Spirit within us.

Holy Water – Water blessed by a religious leader, commonly called "holy water," is often taken home by people as a physical symbol to elicit God's mercy and favor. They are instructed to sprinkle it on objects in their homes. However, people may become anxious if their supply of blessed water runs out, leading them to seek another blessing from the religious leader. In such situations, whether their faith is founded on God or on the physical symbol of holy water is worth considering.

Amulets and Talismans – No matter how fervently

one prays to them and even to the rosary, they cannot replace the guidance of the Holy Spirit.

Though handkerchiefs from the body of Paul were used to perform miracles, this likely occurred only once in his life. Therefore, it is not wise to establish a doctrine based on it or make it a regular practice to have people bring their handkerchiefs to be blessed by a prophet.

Overreliance on these symbols can hinder the growth of faith and a reliance on the Holy Spirit, which is the path to follow under the New Covenant. Therefore, it is the duty of all leaders, in whatever capacity, to teach and lead people to build their knowledge of God and faith in walking with Him.

It is stated in Ezekiel 44:23-24,

And they shall teach My people the difference between the holy and the unholy, and cause them to discern between the unclean and the clean. In controversy they shall stand as judges, and judge it according to My judgments. They shall keep My laws and My statutes in all My appointed meetings, and they shall hallow My Sabbaths.

True prophets are called to provide holistic ministry to believers. They are tasked with teaching people the difference between what is holy and unholy, and discerning what is clean and unclean. They should act as judges in disputes and follow God's laws and statutes in all His appointed meetings, including keeping the Sabbaths holy.

Yet, in our time, many prophets seem to focus solely on predicting future events, neglecting their duty to instruct and guide followers on how to live their lives fully.

This lack of holistic ministry leaves people unprepared and vulnerable. As leaders, we must fulfill our duty and responsibility to those we serve, offering guidance and support to help them grow in their faith and relationship with God.

The way forward

Historians note that in 1936, legendary evangelist and healing minister Smith Wigglesworth prophesied to David du Plessis, a South African-born Pentecostal minister, predicting two significant developments in the universal church: a massive restoration of the gifts of the Holy Spirit, and a revival emphasis on the Word of God.

Wigglesworth added that when these two movements of the Spirit combine, we shall witness the greatest move the church of Jesus Christ has ever seen (cited in Wigglesworth – A Man who Walked with God, by George Stormont, Sovereign World, 1989).

This prophecy by Smith Wigglesworth provides a refreshing insight that the move and manifestation of the gifts of the Holy Spirit must be accompanied by an understanding and application of scripture. God does not leave Himself without a witness wherever His word is declared.

The way forward is to balance the Word and the Spirit. But how do we ensure that Satan does not hijack what Smith Wigglesworth prophesied in 1936?

Jonathan Edwards, a great man of God, provides the keys to understanding the genuine work of the Holy Spirit. In his day, some people, not unlike today, failed to see the Great Awakening or Revival as the work of the Spirit of God. They argued that God is a God of order, as mentioned in 1 Corinthians 14:33 and 40, and therefore the revival was not a genuine work of God. However, the criticisms Edwards received prompted him to write his classic essay "Distinguishing Marks of the Spirit of God" (1741), in which he set forth the criteria for determining the genuine work of the Holy Spirit.

Edwards made the following statements to guide us:

1. The foremost test of the ministry or work is whether it agrees with the teaching of the Holy Scripture. The Scriptures are the standard, not our own particular interpretation of them.

2. Manifestations themselves prove nothing, as scripture does not give us a universal rule to judge these manifestations, though they may or may not be a genuine work of God. An authentic and powerful work of the Holy Spirit can occur without observable physical phenomena.

3. When scripture does not speak directly to a particular issue, the only test for determining a genuine work of God is whether that work manifests the fruit of the Holy Spirit (Matt. 7:16-20). Testing the fruit of our work is absolutely essential in cases where the Scriptures appear to be silent.

4. We should not evaluate something by how bizarre or strange it may seem. "Strange" is not a Scriptural rule determining whether an action or ministry is from God.

5. Suppose we attach great significance to the manifestations (such as nature, trembling, shouting, shaking, etc.). In that case, people may equate the manifestation with the work of the Spirit and even view them as a badge of opportunity. Suppressing manifestation is not the answer; rather, we want to honor the work of the Spirit—convicting, forgiving, saving, healing, and delivering—not the physical reaction to His work.

Purpose of God's Word

Let's clarify the purpose of scripture in the New Testament so that we can identify any deviations. The Apostle Paul makes the purpose clear to us in 2 Timothy 3:16-17:

> *All Scripture is given by inspiration of God, and is profitable for doctrine, for reproof, for correction, for instruction in right-eousness, that the man of God may be complete, thoroughly equipped for every good work.*

According to the word of Paul, scriptures serve five purposes:

1. Doctrine: It reveals the truth about God, Man, and the World, providing answers (Jn. 5:39-47; Rev. 4:11).

2. Reproof: It identifies what we should stop doing, such as sin (Prov. 14:12; 1 Cor. 15:1-13).

3. Correction: It shows us what we should start doing, such as following God's will (Acts 17:10-11; 1 Cor. 16:15; 2 Tim. 2:15).

4. Instruction in Righteousness: It teaches us how to live for God and Christ (Phil. 1:9-11; Heb. 12:11; Eph. 3:17-19).

5. Equipping for every good work (Eph. 2:8-10; Titus 3:5-8).

Righteousness shouldn't be as complicated as our generation makes it out to be. As ministers of God, we should keep three simple things in mind when discussing bearing fruit that matches our repentance, salvation, and the good works that should follow (John 15:1-6).

The apostolic father, St. Augustine, simplified righteousness by breaking it down into three components:

1. Our actions (what we do)

2. The motivation behind our actions (why we do it)

3. The manner in which we carry out our actions. (how we do it)

These three components encapsulate everything we do in the name of The Lord and His Kingdom.

While the ministry of the Prophet is powerful and essential, it cannot stand alone. People need more than just knowledge of future events; they must also prepare themselves for what may come.

Thankfully, God, in His wisdom, did not limit the ministry gifts within the body to the Prophet. As Paul wrote in Ephesians 4, all the ministry gifts work together to bless God's children.

Chapter 9

Recognize your Humanity

If you lose touch with your humanity, you lose everything." - Marcus Aurelius

As we navigate these end-times, a looming danger threatens to sink even the most seasoned of prophets – the risk of losing touch with their own humanity. It is an ever-present peril that must be met with steadfast vigilance and unwavering resolve.

To fulfill their divine mandate, prophets must be acutely aware of the critical duty to keep this truth at the forefront of their minds. They must never forget that they are human, subject to the same frailties and limitations as any other mortal being. Only by acknowledging this fundamental fact can they hope to remain grounded and connected to the people they are called to serve.

As discussed elsewhere in this book, the office of the Prophet is unique because it is the only office through which people generally believe God speaks directly to them. Unfortunately, this perception often creates a perilous situation where people begin to hail the Prophet and lavish accolades fit for a deity upon him. Tragically, some prophets revel in this elevated status, the genesis of trouble.

It is important to recall that even Jesus refused to give in to the people's pressure to crown Him as King when He walked the earth. He is the King of kings, and He did not require anyone to anoint Him as such. In fact, Jesus frequently found a way to slip out of the people's sight in most moments.

It is a timeless truth that human beings constantly seek to connect with God. If God was not Spirit and was instead human like us, one can only imagine the throngs of people that would gather anywhere He went, much like they did with Jesus. The natural tendency for people to attach themselves to someone they perceive as powerful is a reality that will endure as long as humanity exists.

This is the two-edged sword of the identity and office of the Prophet. On the one hand, the Prophet has been anointed with a divine calling and profound spiritual authority.

Yet, on the other hand, the Prophet must come to terms with the fact that they are human, with all the limitations and frailties that come with that reality. Only by embracing this truth can the Prophet hope to navigate the treacherous waters of their calling and avoid the pitfalls of self-aggrandizement and delusions of grandeur.

Humility

Humility is the key to avoiding being deified by followers. Humble individuals acknowledge God in every moment of their lives, recognizing that God has made them what they are, and without God, they are nothing.

They are always mindful of giving God the glory. If people attempt to elevate them beyond measure, they promptly correct and rebuke them if necessary.

However, some individuals enjoy the adoration from followers until it spirals out of control. One of the hallmarks of humility is acknowledging your mistakes when they are pointed out. Prophets, especially those new to the office, may make mistakes. Even those who have held the office for some time may err, emphasizing that our knowledge is incomplete. As Paul clearly explains in 1 Corinthinians 13:9, *"For we know in part, and we prophesy in part."*

Hananiah Prophesied a Lie

Let me use the narrative about Hananiah, the Prophet, to make a point here. Here's Hananiah's story in **Jeremiah 28:2-6**

> *Thus speaks the Lord of hosts, the God of Israel, saying: 'I have broken the yoke of the King of Babylon. Within two full years I will bring back to this place all the vessels of the Lord's house, that Nebuchadnezzar king of Babylon took away from this place and carried to Babylon.*
>
> *And I will bring back to this place Jeconiah the son of Jehoiakim, King of Judah, with all the captives of Judah who*

*went to Babylon,' says the Lord, 'for I will break the yoke of the
king of Babylon.' "*

*Then the Prophet Jeremiah spoke to the Prophet Hananiah
in the presence of the priests and in the presence of all the people
who stood in the house of the Lord, and the Prophet Jeremiah
said,*

*"Amen! The Lord do so; the Lord perform your words which
you have prophesied, to bring back the vessels of the Lord's house
and all who were carried away captive, from Babylon to this
place.*

The scripture verse above contains a prophecy given by
Hananiah in the presence of Jeremiah. Jeremiah initially
accepted the prophecy as being from the Lord.

However, later God revealed to Jeremiah that the prophecy
was false. Jeremiah then prophesied that Hananiah would face
God's judgment, which came to pass as Jeremiah had predicted
in Jeremiah 28:15-17:

*Then the Prophet Jeremiah said to Hananiah the Prophet, "Hear
now, Hananiah, the Lord has not sent you, but you make this
people trust in a lie.*

*Therefore thus says the Lord: 'Behold, I will cast you from
the face of the earth. This year you shall die, because you have
taught rebellion against the Lord.' " So Hananiah the Prophet
died the same year in the seventh month.*

There is an essential lesson to learn from this story, as the
tragic outcome could have been avoided. Even Jeremiah initially

believed that Hananiah's prophecy came from the Lord, indicating that both prophets were mistaken.

This underscores the importance of exercising good judgment. As earlier scriptures teach, if a prophet gives a false prophecy, they should no longer be alive to continue deceiving people. Sadly, this is what happened to Hananiah.

The Humanity in Old Testament Prophets

The significant lesson is that prophets, like all humans, are subject to the flesh and can make mistakes.

Abraham lied twice. For instance, Abraham, a man of God who left his family to follow God's voice to an unknown land, lied twice about Sarah, his wife. First, in Genesis 12:12, he asked Sarah to say she was his sister to protect himself from potential harm.

> *Therefore it will happen, when the Egyptians see you, that they will say, 'This is his wife'; and they will kill me, but they will let you live. Please say you are my sister, that it may be well with me for your sake, and that I may live because of you.*

In Genesis 20:1-3, he repeated the same mistake, and God had to intervene to prevent harm from coming to Sarah.

> *And Abraham journeyed from there to the South, and dwelt between Kadesh and Shur, and stayed in Gerar. Now Abraham said of Sarah his wife, "She is my sister." And Abimelech king of Gerar sent and took Sarah. But God came to Abimelech in a dream by night, and said to him, "Indeed you are a dead man*

because of the woman whom you have taken, for she is a man's wife."

You are reading about a man, widely regarded as a prophet, who obeyed God's call to leave his family and homeland, journeyed to an unfamiliar land, and was declared by God to be the Father of many nations.

Yet, despite his remarkable faith, he faltered and lied twice. Thankfully, God intervened in both instances and set things right.

Elijah wished for his own death. Another example of a prophet's humanity is Elijah's fear-driven request for death. Despite having prophesied years of drought and famine to Israel because of their rebellion against God, Elijah was overcome with fear when Baal was worshiped, and false prophets took over Israel.

As a result, he went into the wilderness and prayed that God would take his life, saying he was no better than his fathers. Such a display of faithlessness and despair raises the question of what might have happened had Elijah taken his own life.

This incident is recorded in 1 Kings 19:4, where we read,

But he himself went a day's journey into the wilderness, and came and sat down under a broom tree. And he prayed that he might die, and said, 'It is enough! Now, LORD, take my life, for I am no better than my fathers!'

Despite his faltering faith, God came to his rescue.

Balaam followed the love of money. Balaam was offered gifts to prophesy against Israel, despite God's warnings not to do so. God had to intervene by speaking through Balaam's donkey, something that had never happened before or since.

Numbers 22:32-33 recounts how the Angel of the Lord stood against Balaam, saying,

> *Why have you struck your donkey these three times? Behold, I have come out to stand against you, because your way is perverse before Me.*
>
> *The donkey saw Me and turned aside from Me these three times. If she had not turned aside from Me, surely I would also have killed you by now, and let her live.*

Balaam's actions were driven by greed, and he attempted to curse a people whom God had blessed. Yet, despite his misguided intentions, God intervened once again.

Jonah was angry with God. Yet, despite Jonah's reluctance, he ultimately carried out God's directive to preach to Nineveh, resulting in the repentance of the city's population and the avoidance of their impending judgment.

Nevertheless, Jonah was furious with God for sparing Nineveh, as he believed they deserved to be punished for their sins. This is evident in Jonah 4:1-3.

> *But it displeased Jonah exceedingly, and he became angry. So he prayed to the Lord, and said, "Ah, Lord, was not this what I said when I was still in my country?*
>
> *Therefore I fled previously to Tarshish; for I know that You are a gracious and merciful God, slow to anger and abundant in lovingkindness, One who relents from doing*

harm. Therefore now, O Lord, please take my life from me, for it is better for me to die than to live!

Two Realities

As Christians, we exist in two realities. The first is that despite being saved from Adam's disobedience, our old nature persists and constantly struggles against our spirit. This is a lower reality.

However, there is also a higher reality: we are new creations in Christ and can accomplish all things through His strength. The Apostle John states that those born of God do not continue to sin, yet he also acknowledges that if we confess our sins, God will forgive and cleanse us.

The examples cited above illustrate the lower reality of believers. Although they were not false prophets and were called by God, their stories demonstrate that even prophets are human and subject to their fleshly desires at times. This is where humility comes into play.

If one assumes they are infallible as a prophet, they are putting themselves in a dangerous position. God will not excuse leading people astray through selfish or fleshly tendencies simply because someone is a prophet.

The spirit of the Prophet is subject to the Prophet, but the Holy Spirit remains above both the Prophet and their human spirit. Therefore, it is essential to embrace humility, no matter how anointed others believe you to be.

The Character of the Prophet

The Bible discusses God's bestowal of spiritual gifts to believers in two forms: the gifts of the Spirit (1 Corinthians 14) and the fruit of the Spirit (Galatians 5:22-24).

Historically, people have focused on the gifts of the Spirit, as they are more visible and easier to identify. As a result, one often hears about how gifted someone is before learning about their character.

However, the New Testament prophet who desires to be successful in their ministry must pay as much attention to the fruit of the Spirit as they do to the gift of God upon their life. It is important to remember that the anointing comes from one source – the Holy Spirit. Thus, the Holy Spirit will not bestow a great gift and leave one with questionable character and life-style. If you are anointed and your gift is greater than your character, you are in trouble.

Jesus aptly taught that false prophets would be recognized by their fruit. The fruit of the Spirit cannot be faked; one's character is either good or bad, regardless of their gift. Therefore, when the Word of God states that the spirits of the prophets are subject to the prophets, it refers to personal discipline in exercising God's gift.

As a prophet, it is crucial to work on your character. Take time to meditate on the passage from the Apostle Peter found in 2 Peter 1:1-9.

Simon Peter, a bondservant and Apostle of Jesus Christ, to those who have obtained like precious faith with us by the righteousness of our God and Savior Jesus Christ:

Grace and peace be multiplied to you in the knowledge of God and of Jesus our Lord, as His divine power has given to us all things that pertain to life and godliness, through the knowledge of Him who called us by glory and virtue,

by which have been given to us exceedingly great and precious promises, that through these you may be partakers of the divine nature, having escaped the corruption that is in the world through lust.

But also for this very reason, giving all diligence, add to your faith virtue, to virtue knowledge, to knowledge self-control, to self-control perseverance, to perseverance godliness, to godliness brotherly kindness, and to brotherly kindness love.

For if these things are yours and abound, you will be neither barren nor unfruitful in the knowledge of our Lord Jesus Christ. For he who lacks these things is shortsighted, even to blindness, and has forgotten that he was cleansed from his old sins.

Beware of the Gehazi Syndrome

There are several crucial lessons to be learned from Gehazi's story and his association with the Prophet Elisha. One could argue that Prophet Elisha failed to teach Gehazi the value of integrity, as evidenced by the lessons found in 2 Kings 5:20-22.

But Gehazi, the servant of Elisha the man of God, said, "Look, my master has spared Naaman this Syrian, while not receiving from his hands what he brought; but as the Lord lives, I will run after him and take something from him." So Gehazi pursued Naaman.

When Naaman saw him running after him, he got down from the chariot to meet him, and said, "Is all well?" And he said, "All is well. My master has sent me, saying, 'Indeed, just now two young men of the sons of the prophets have come to me from the mountains of Ephraim. Please give them a talent of silver and two changes of garments.'

The Prophet Elisha had prayed for Naaman to be healed of leprosy. Naaman offered gifts to the Man of God, but Elisha declined to receive them. Instead, he only did what God anointed him to do – minister to people in need and improve their lives.

However, Gehazi, Elisha's servant, acting out of greed and covetousness went behind his master's back to pursue Naaman and collect the gifts that Elisha had declined. He then lied to his master about his actions and paid dearly for his behavior, as seen in 2 Kings 5:25-27.

Now he went in and stood before his master. Elisha said to him, "Where did you go, Gehazi?" And he said, "Your servant did not go anywhere."

Then he said to him, "Did not my heart go with you when the man turned back from his chariot to meet you? Is it time to receive money and to receive clothing, olive groves and vineyards, sheep and oxen, male and female servants?

Therefore the leprosy of Naaman shall cling to you and your descendants forever." And he went out from his presence leprous, as white as snow.

For his greed, Gehazi inherited the sickness that Naaman

was healed from. One would have expected that after several years of serving Elisha, Gehazi would have developed character, but he did not.

Unfortunately, many people who follow older prophets can fall victim to greed and a desire for popularity if that is all they see about being a prophet.

Four Areas of Integrity Where Gehazi Failed, and We Must Watch:

When you start viewing your ministry as a lucrative business (2 Kings 5:19-20). Gehazi saw his master, Elisha, as a fool because he allowed an opportunity to make it big slip through his hands. To Gehazi, religion was big business.

However, you cannot commodify the anointing; it is not a means of making money. You must serve even those who cannot offer anything tangible in return for the impact your ministry has on their lives.

When you begin to see people (church members) as gullible, naive customers. Gehazi demonstrated this attitude towards Naaman when he called him "this Syrian" with disdain. So many people come to church seeking an experience with God that can change their circumstances in life.

They may need emotional healing or direction in their lives. The church should be a place of healing and refreshment for those struggling in life, and it's essential not to take advantage of them.

When you begin to see God as a "silent part-

ner." In Gehazi's case, he said, "But as the LORD lives, I will run after him and take something from him" (2 Kings 5:20b).

This decision did not come from God. Instead, Gehazi saw God as a "silent partner" whose input did not matter. Never think that you can make decisions on behalf of God, and that He must move along with you. God is not a silent partner in your ministry, but He is the One who should lead and direct you in all your dealings.

When you begin to argue that the end justifies the means. (2 Kings 5:21-22) In Christian ethics, it is unacceptable to justify immoral or unethical behavior based on achieving a desired outcome.

Gehazi attempted to justify stealing from Naaman by planning to give some of the ill-gotten gains to the sons of the prophets. However, stealing cannot be justified by any good intention, and Gehazi was still held accountable for his wrongdoing.

Steps to follow for maintaining integrity

- Recognize that as a human, you are prone to mistakes in your words, attitudes, and actions.
- Be quick to admit and apologize for any wrongdoing, seeking forgiveness and restoration with God and others.
- Be willing to apologize to anyone, including those who look up to you, if necessary.

- Regularly examine yourself and your faith, remembering that you will one day give an account of yourself to God.
- Consistently direct the attention of your listeners and followers toward the Lord Jesus in all that you do and speak.

In a world where integrity is often sacrificed for personal gain and success, it is crucial to be intentional about maintaining it. As you follow these steps, may you always remember that true success is not measured by the size of your following or the fame you attain but by your faithfulness to God and His call on your life.

May your integrity shine as a beacon of hope to those around you, and may your ministry leave a lasting impact beyond your earthly existence. May the Lord strengthen and guide

Epilogue- My Prayer for You

My dear friend, as I pray for you, my heart is filled with hope and expectation for the amazing things God has in store for your life. I pray that nothing hinders the anointing of the Holy Spirit upon your life and that you may fully embrace the calling God has placed upon you.

May you be a shining example of Christ in everything you do and in every encounter you have with those around you. May the love of God shine brightly through you, bringing healing and hope to those who need it most.

I pray that your ministry as a prophet will continue to grow and flourish, touching the lives of countless individuals, even beyond your earthly existence. May your message continue to resonate with those who hear it, inspiring them to draw closer to God and to live out their faith with boldness and conviction.

May God continue to bless you and guide you on this journey of faith, and may you always remember that you are never alone. May His presence be with you every step of the way, and may you always find strength and courage in His love and grace.

So go forth, my friend, and live out your calling with passion and purpose. May your life be a testament to the power of God's love and the transformation that can happen when we surrender ourselves fully to His will. May you always remember that with God, all things are possible and that through Him, you can accomplish anything that He has called you to do.

Archbishop Nicholas Duncan-Williams

With over four decades of Ministry behind him, Archbishop Nicholas Duncan-Williams is the Presiding Archbishop and General Overseer of Action Chapel International (ACI), head-quartered in Accra, Ghana, and United Denominations of Action Chapel International, which has over 150 affiliates and branch churches located in North America, Europe, Asia, and Africa.

Archbishop Duncan-Williams is also the Founder and Chairman of Nicholas Duncan-Williams Ministries (formerly Prayer Summit International), which hosts prayer summits around the globe, bringing revival to international cities through corporate and intercessory prayer and training.

With a unique anointing in prayer and intercession, Archbishop is recognized by many leaders in the body of Christ as the "Apostle of Strategic Prayer."

Having gained accreditation and respect from recognized church leaders, God has used him to counsel and speak into the lives of world leaders while still maintaining his touch with the everyday person. As a result, he is affectionately called "Papa" by many.

More Classics by Archbishop Nicholas Duncan-Williams

Available through Amazon.com

- Prayer Moves God
- Enforcing Prophetic Decrees Vol. 1, 2, & 3
- Gratitude
- Power Behind the Scenes
- Binding the Strong Man
- Understanding the Father Factor
- Praying the Promises of God
- Providence and Destiny
- The Prayer Journal – Enforcing God's Mandate for My Life
- Turning Pain to Power
- Don't Fight the Process
- Understanding the End Time: Sounding the Trumpet of Readiness to the End Time Church

When you join One Million Strong, you will gain instant access to:

- **Financial Freedom Prayer Declaration**
- **Discover the Secrets to Effective Prayer** Course
- **Breakthrough in the Spiritual Realm** Audio

Made in the USA
Middletown, DE
08 July 2024

56914338R00082